Apple pie beds and eggy bread

An affectionate memoir of boarding school life

DIANE M. LANGDON

Apple pie beds and eggy bread

An affectionate memoir of boarding school life

DIANE M. LANGDON

MEREO
Cirencester

Mereo Books

1A The Wool Market Dyer Street Cirencester Gloucestershire GL7 2PR
An imprint of Memoirs Publishing www.mereobooks.com

Apple-pie beds and eggy bread: 978-1-86151-508-7

First published in Great Britain in 2015
by Mereo Books, an imprint of Memoirs Publishing

Copyright ©2015

The address for Memoirs Publishing Group Limited can be found at
www.memoirspublishing.com

The Memoirs Publishing Group Ltd Reg. No. 7834348

The Memoirs Publishing Group supports both The Forest Stewardship Council® (FSC®) and the
PEFC® leading international forest-certification organisations. Our books carrying both the FSC
label and the PEFC® and are printed on FSC®-certified paper. FSC® is the only
forest-certification scheme supported by the leading environmental organisations including
Greenpeace. Our paper procurement policy can be found at
www.memoirspublishing.com/environment

Typeset in 10/16pt Century Schoolbook
by Wiltshire Associates Publisher Services Ltd. Printed and bound in Great Britain by
Printondemand-Worldwide, Peterborough PE2 6XD

CONTENTS

Preface

PREFACE

I hope you enjoy this personal account of what it was like for me as a pupil at Fyfield County Boarding School in the late 1960s. I have tried to include some further interest by adding one or two personal stories from people who I am still in touch with. I loved reading about their journeys, as they were complementary to my own.

Of course, not everyone's experience was the same as mine, far from it, but there will be elements that are quite similar. Where possible I have tried to leave names out to save anyone's embarrassment. If I have dates wrong, then you can be assured that all the events took place in the years 1965 to 1970.

It was when I was researching the history of Fyfield that I learned some amazing facts that I hope, you too, will find fascinating. I won't spoil it for you by telling you what they are here.

I'm glad there was a slight delay in publishing this book, because it has enabled me to thank the Brentwood Gazette for superb coverage of the clock restoration project and individuals' responses to their article. It is lovely to know that the new residents of the Fyfield site respect its history and have been so accommodating to the alumni. It has forged a good community friendship. I hope that they too will find my book worth a read. The Fyfield site, now called Elmbridge Hall, has such a good feel to it, and every time I return there it feels somehow special.

I also hope that some parents who read this understand that it was neither cruel nor thoughtless to 'pack your child off to boarding school'. It was in fact a privilege and the opportunity of a lifetime to be able to attend Fyfield. Besides providing me with good life skills, it has given me very happy memories and long-lasting friendships to treasure all my life.

My special thanks go to those who contributed by writing about their experience and those who provided me with photographs. I am grateful, as I think this has helped to shape the book.

I love meeting up with my 'Fyfield Family', I love hearing about them and their families and experiences, and we are all there for one another in times of difficulties too. Long may it continue.

Chapter One

IN THE BEGINNING

When I first decided to write a book, I thought I would set something out in chronological order, but the more I thought about it, the more I realised that my school years were a series of events in no particular order and an account of how things were in the 1960s.

A lot changed during that decade. I was a baby boomer. A baby boom is of course a surge in the birth rate, generally associated with optimism and a period of sustained economic growth. Roughly speaking, this one began just after the Second World War and ended in the mid-1960s. I was glad that my birth was associated with optimism and economic growth, because the only way was up for both me and all those of the same age. That was good news for us born in the East End of London, as life had been pretty grim at times, what with outside lavatories, tin baths, no central heating, second-hand clothes and more than our fair share of serious illnesses. We tried to be happy despite abject poverty.

Through a decade from the 1950s to the 1960s we saw ourselves as the emerging 'new' class because despite conditions, everything was improving. My parents owned their own home in London, a telephone, a gramophone and a motor bike with side car, all by the age of 21. This was primarily due to the fact that nothing much was available to buy either during or shortly after the war, both of them had been working since they were 14-15 and they were both living at home until they married. By the time I went to Fyfield they owned a car, had built an 'indoor bathroom', were going to see opera and, to the dismay of most of my family, some with communist sympathies, had joined the local Conservative Club. My dad said it was just because they had a better piano than the Labour lot, but nobody wanted to believe him. So you might guess that I was brought up amidst lively conversations, opinions, colourful language and laughter. Nothing was ever dull in our household! It was always busy too, with lots of activity and lots of visitors.

How I came to attend Fyfield County Boarding School was strange in itself. It all started one day while I was a pupil at a junior school called Stoneydown Park.

In the 1960s, Stoneydown Park was a small, newly-built, modern junior school adjacent to a pretty little park, a place where I spent some considerable amount of time. It was in the East End of London, Walthamstow (E17). I was the first pupil to enter through the gates of this school, and my classroom was to one side of a pretty courtyard. In contrast to the school I had left, an old Victorian building with outside toilets, this was an airy and welcoming paradise. It was a beautiful new building with huge panoramic windows that let in plenty of light, lovely new wooden floors, a new gymnasium, big light classrooms and new desks and chairs. Best of all were lovely and welcoming teachers. We had been fortunate to have teachers that wanted to teach and who were enthusiastic, inspiring and caring. Gone were the teachers who thought if they shouted loudly, you might glean some education.

We played on the swings in the adjacent park during all of our breaks, called 'playtime', which were often extended when it was a lovely day. There was a mix of children from lots of other schools, so there was plenty of opportunity to make new friends. It was only a couple of minutes' walk from home with no busy roads to cross either, unlike my previous school, where every day you diced with death crossing very busy roads and despite there being a zebra crossing, it was touch and go whether or not motorists stopped.

The time at Stoneydown Park Junior School went all too fast, but it was both memorable and fun. To this day I can remember a number of things about this school, such as having very large bookcases in each classroom stacked with brand new books, going to swimming lessons (which was new to me), and each of us sitting cross-legged having our hair towel-dried one by one by our teacher. The endless sun streamed into the small courtyard, which had a little fountain with the sound of the trickling water. I made lots of friends at this school, but there are three I am still in contact with, over half a century later.

One day during my last year at this school, a speaker came to talk to us about 'going up to senior school', what was expected and what was going to happen after leaving junior school. When you are ten, even eleven seems a long way off, especially when summer holidays loom. Not that I was concentrating much on the future, but we were told that some of us would go to the local grammar school, if they passed the eleven plus, some would go to boarding school and most would go to a secondary modern school. During the talk, it was explained what our expectations were likely to be. Those who went to grammar school were likely to be academic and eventually professional in some capacity, and would have to work very hard and stay on at school well beyond the age of 15, the school-leaving age at the time. They were also likely to be boys and not girls. It was also hinted that our parents knew who these pupils were, and that it was not for us to decide. Girls were expected to get married and become mothers, so we would possibly have jobs until we got married. That was how it was in the mid-sixties. We were also told that those who were lucky enough to go to boarding school would be taught to stand on their own two feet and most importantly could enjoy a range of sporting and outdoor activities, and the rest, who went to the secondary modern schools, would do 'ordinary jobs' in life, whatever that meant. That was it - your future decided at age 11! It seemed it would be a secondary modern for most of us, but it sounded more like fate than a future.

I had no idea whatsoever about working life. I had no idea what constituted an 'ordinary job'. I had started infant school aged four years and one month old (the youngest), and now I was ten.

My father worked with students at Walthamstow Technical College during the day and at Whipps Cross hospital during the evenings. He was a Senior Laboratory Technician in the Mechanical and Production Engineering Department during the day and did a job in the evenings at hospital. He rewired houses during the weekends. He also took wedding photographs and developed them in a cupboard at home on Saturdays. Prior to this he owned a photographic shop until he was persuaded by his family to get a proper job, and that was when he went to work at the local technical college. So I had some idea about what he did.

My mother was at home all day and did a bit of housework, tons of laundry and shopping, cooked meals and looked after the family, which was the four of us, Mum, Dad and my little brother Jeff, who was fifteen months younger than me. I really had little idea of what this entailed, except I remember part of it was going to the baby clinic to get very large tins of National Dried baby milk, as I was taken along to this too because I was neither observant nor appreciative. Both my nans had worked, one in the film industry, which she had started during the Second World War, as she spoke Italian and some German. My granddad was a milkman and then later a window cleaner for a toy shop. The other nan worked in a laundry in Leyton, East London, to begin with and later was an accountant at a local knitwear factory, but in addition to this she made boxes at home, all of which jobs had been in order to support her, my granddad and the family. My granddad had been very ill, housebound an not working, and he died by the time I was nine years old, so although I knew a little about both my nans' jobs, I had thought I would stay at home and be like Mum. It seemed a good option at the time.

Work seemed so far away, so my interest in it was zero. Although I had earned some money doing odd jobs and singing in a choir I had no idea about living expenses and bills. I just thought that money was spent on sweets and presents for family, as you did at ten years old and without access to the media in the sixties. In most ways I was very young for my age and as reading fiction was my number one hobby, you might say I was fanciful or dreamy as well. In my mind I lived entirely in another, more adventurous world.

Anyway, to get back to the school talk, I immediately liked the sound of 'standing on your own two feet', which had a feel of neither having to work hard or having to do an ordinary job, both of which appealed to me at the age of ten. The outdoor element of the talk about boarding school I found particularly appealing. I was blissfully unaware of anything beyond the next four or five years of school.

So I went home to talk to Mum and Dad and told them what we had been told at school. They laughed and said that nothing had changed that much since they were at secondary school, except you had to stay on until fifteen and we weren't well off enough for me to have grand ideas of boarding school, so I shouldn't keep my nose in books about them either. I was an avid reader from a very early age, and by this time I had exhausted the whole Mallory Towers series, despite my Dad telling me that fiction was overrated and lending me his Norton motorcycle manual, which he said was what a proper book was all about.

My Dad had enjoyed school and learning as he had soaked up knowledge. He seemed to know most things. He had taught himself how to play the piano and about photography, and had set up his own dark room in the cupboard. He was passionate about motor bikes, which he regularly stripped down on the sitting room floor (this was until he and Mum were no longer on speaking terms, when he would move it all out to the hallway). He rewired houses and he had built a new bathroom and kitchen, all before he reached the age of thirty.

Mum on the other hand was at the opposite end of the spectrum, for her school had been a total waste of time. She never liked school, teachers or subjects other than embroidery. She told me that one of the best days of her life was when she left school. To her school was something you just had to grin, bear and get through it. It would have suited her not to have gone to school. It had been a matter of survival for her. She didn't like work that much either. She liked my Dad, dancing, the radiogram, motorbikes, painting her very long fingernails scarlet and reading second-hand magazines. I remember her telling me she hated rules and that was the real problem with both school and work. She once told me that rules were made to be broken and gave the people who made them something worthwhile to do with their time. That was probably the reason we didn't have many, if any, rules at our house! It was also the reason I started to become responsible at such a young age: making sure the fire guard was on, checking doors were locked, checking that the gas cooker was turned off, especially after over hearing talk about how Sylvia Plath had died. Apparently I also used to lecture people on why all these things had to be done, and had a whole range of facial expressions to go with each activity.

So with no joy of any advice or discussion at home about boarding school, I decided to go to the local library and speak to the librarian, who was knowledgeable and who I considered my elderly friend. She knew me very well as one of the library's younger regular users. I was three when I joined the library and started to borrow books. I remember her bending the rules to allow me to take out more books than was 'officially allowed'. She gave me an adult library card too, by being my sponsor, as she trusted me with books. I probably spent more time at the library than anywhere else, except church. I told her about my dream of wanting to go to a boarding school and what my parents had said about it, and she said she would do some research on the subject and if I went in the next week with my Mum and Dad we could have a chat.

Next week couldn't come soon enough! Off I went to the library, dragging my parents along too, just in case they thought it another one of my fanciful episodes, and I had managed to get a written note from the Librarian. We spoke to a lady who said 'I have found out that if you want to apply for an assisted place at an authority-run school, you can'. She explained to my parents that the education was free and only boarding fees had to be paid, and you could apply for money towards this too. She then passed over a big bundle of information, including the application forms. My parents took the information pack and said we would discuss it at home.

By this time my parents had a good handle on my perseverance, reminding me that I'd inherited that trait from Maud, my Nan, who had a good sense of humour, was hardworking, and had a wonderful grasp of finance and long-held communist tendencies. She never had much of a temper except for where there was injustice, when she blew. Nobody ever frightened her and she was never in awe of anyone. She taught me all I ever needed to know about equality and council officials. At that age I couldn't see the similarities with myself, but time would tell that my parents were fairly accurate in their observations.

I was qualified to apply for the three state-run local boarding schools because I was born and lived in the vicinity that allowed this, North East West Ham or Newham, part of Tower Hamlets, as it is now known. During the 50s and 60s Newham was one of the most deprived and overpopulated areas of London, so I realised that competition to get to a boarding school was going to be strong.

Following our discussions (a discussion in my immediate family was where everyone talked loudly, nobody listened to anyone else, everyone thought that their point was the best one and everyone was satisfied with the outcome), my parents decided to consult 'the wider family', as all good East End families tended to do in those days. This was primarily because it was an important decision and my parents had only just turned thirty years old, so I expect they wanted some family reassurance, not to mention financial help. The family thought it was a very good idea, as it might broaden my horizons beyond books and singing! It would also possibly 'keep me out of trouble' - not that I understood this, because I'd never really been in trouble. To my mind there was a very limited amount of trouble at church and in books. Mind you, I didn't really understand much about the way adults thought. I just accepted that they probably knew best. My Nan's opinion was that fresh country air would benefit my health, and for that reason alone it was a very good idea to send me into the depths of the Essex countryside. Frankly she had probably had enough of nursing me with polio, scarlet fever, measles, endless bouts of croup and every other illness I had the misfortune of acquiring in the smoggy capital. Later this would prove that again my Nan's judgement had been spot on.

Most importantly, if it was what I wanted then why not? That is the very good thing about a close-knit family, they were always optimistic, positive and found ways of achieving what was desired. The application to Fyfield County Boarding School was made.

The family were close knit, partly because of the Second World War. Mum's family were predominantly Belgian, while Dad's were Prussian (German/Polish) and Italian. Both their families lived in a couple of streets in London, and they had all been through a lot together. In fact most of my family, one way or another, lived in Beaumont Road or Sophia Road, Leyton. When one house had been bombed they moved in with the next nearest relative or friends of the same nationality (foreign or non-indigenous counted as a nationality) until at the end of the war they were all so overcrowded - and it stayed that way until they were all were married or rehoused - that I hadn't got a clue who I was directly related to. I think they could have qualified for the Guinness Book of Records for how many people can live in a house at any one time and not get on each other's nerves.

Considering neither my mother nor father had any brothers or sisters, I had a huge number of aunties and uncles. Not only that but I never really got to know anybody's real name, because everyone had a nickname or a derivative of their own name. Oddly enough too they predominantly spoke English, but with a lot of their own language thrown in for good measure. I grew up thinking that *bellissimo* (lovely) and *mój skarb* (my treasure) were English words! But I loved and trusted them all and they all adored me.

I must explain that throughout my life I have been a very determined person. I started with this determination at an early age of seven, by going to Walthamstow Swimming Baths, where I taught myself to swim without

11

any help from anyone. It only took ten months of spluttering around in the chlorinated waters of the baths with red demon eyes and a small, faded, shrunken turquoise swimming costume before I became a fairly proficient swimmer. Well, the costume was turquoise when I started to learn, but it was almost white by the time I was competent.

I went with a friend called Jeanne, and day after day for weeks on end we learnt to swim. This was supplemented by my Dad taking me to Whipps Cross Lido and Larkswood Lido every Friday evening. We went to these open-air pools irrespective of the weather - often it was raining. We swam with the inner tubes of his bike tyre blown up, just in case I needed a float, but by the time we had been there for the first year I was using the diving board.

At four I had already started my own business, albeit small, running errands for people, most of which earned a few pence a go and occasionally sixpence. My most lucrative market was returning the stout empties to the off licence to get returns money and pick up the new order, which I did on my three-wheeled bike, which had an attached boot bin. Every time I went into the 'offy' the publican used to say, 'Look out her she comes, Sunshine Shirley, for her stout'. There weren't any rules about giving alcohol to children to transport and deliver in those days, or if there were they were not adhered to.

My next achievement was when I was seven and got myself into St Michael's and All Angels church choir. It was very busy, with up to five weddings a week, occasional christenings and special services. This provided one of my sources of income during 1961. I was dedicated. I knew by heart everything we sang and became top of the class in religious studies, and I also knew a plethora of Latin religious words. I took it all very seriously.

Building on this, I was making two pounds a month, which I considered not bad for an eight-year-old in 1962! It was very handy too that Jewish people kept me employed from Friday after school and throughout Saturday. I never spent the money as there wasn't really anything I wanted to buy, but I did love to have a chat with all my customers. The Jewish people always felt the need to feed me too and provide me with enough sweets for the week. I took financial advice from Nan, who sensibly opened a National Investment Account for me at the local post office. My income had risen substantially by 1965. I never intended it to be a business, but my regular customers were offended if I refused to take anything and I was always told to save it for a rainy day. My life was full of sunny days at this time.

I continued to carry out these jobs until I was ten and a half, and was so very fortunate to eventually be offered a place at Fyfield County Boarding School. I say eventually because after my initial interview I wasn't offered a place, but went on their reserve list as the first reserve. This meant that if anyone did not take up their place or left, I would secure it. This was not to be in the first school term in September, but during the second term just before Easter.

Until then, I went to the local secondary modern school. It was awful beyond belief. I realised that I wasn't going to survive four years of that school, but I just hoped and prayed that something would change. I wondered why it was called a secondary modern (it was locally known as the William McScruffy) because it was the ugliest-looking Victorian building you could imagine, with many classrooms at subterranean level, and I also wondered why it was called a school at all, because I learnt very little. Lessons were boring and made up of things I already knew or had little interest in, such as reading out loud the simplest of books, doing joined-up handwriting practice, 'times tables' and adding up, taking away and long division, all of which were considered good basic arithmetic, together with cooking and needlework. Most of these things I could already do, having been taught by my family, mostly my Nan. Very occasionally this was supplemented by something a bit more interesting, such as nature study or writing stories.

I was bullied by pupils and teachers alike. You could say I was just naive, but smoking at eleven was quite common, as was stealing any belongings including lunch money. Using threatening behaviour and getting beaten up if you were small was the norm in 1965 in the East End of London.

I was dared by my peers to shoplift fags and declined to accept the dare, so I was ostracised from that moment on. I had my coat stolen, my shoes, my bag and everything in it and my lunch money too. I was physically attacked more times than I could remember. I wanted to be accepted but not at any cost, so I became and remained a loner at this school. In fact the only thing that school taught me that was useful was to run fast, very fast, interspersed with the odd high vault over a garden fence.

I was caned and ridiculed by my male form teacher practically every day in front of the whole class, because I just couldn't or wouldn't speak up for myself. I was the easiest target. Corporal punishment was allowed for even small misdemeanours in school. I regularly got a cane across the hands for being late for class, despite just being the last in the queue, because I was unable to push in further up the line. It was the new teacher's ritual. He strutted about in his nylon tracksuit, ready to pounce. The last two pupils in the line had the cane for not being smart enough to get to the front. It was always the smallest two girls, of whom I was one. I later found that I was not the only person who had suffered. Not that this made the situation any better, but it was some consolation to know that there were very many others who were treated the same and like me hated that school and were, through new technology, able to at least vent their feelings.

It was a good day when in 1987 corporal punishment was abolished. I was beginning to appreciate why my mother hadn't taken to secondary school. I detested that school with a passion.

I was the unhappiest little girl. At this time my family and parents were very worried about me because I used to return home quiet, with bruised fingers. Ridiculously enough, I even got caned across the fingers for not being able to hold a pen because I had been previously caned. Although I never uttered a word about my unhappiness, they knew something was wrong. I don't know why I never told anyone, but I suppose it wasn't right to tell tales. My Dad had said to me that it was high time I learnt to stick up for myself. He gave me a note to take to school to tell them that if I returned home once more injured, he would be visiting the school to dispense his own justice. From that moment on the caning stopped, and I became totally invisible and ignored. I sat at the very back of the class and my name was even left out of registration. It was as if I no longer existed. I hated school and I hated teachers.

However, I knew that something good might turn up. I had a feeling. I had faith.

When a letter arrived saying I was to start at Fyfield County Boarding School for the next term, I thought my prayers had been answered. In preparation for this my parents wrote a letter for me to take to school to explain why I was leaving. I never even bothered to go into that school again, but went walkabout for the week. The letter was never delivered. I posted it down the drain on my way to the school, just before I had got to the gate and I had decided not to finish my last week there. I had also calculated that the truant officer would not call at our house until well after I'd gone to my dream school. I thought the school didn't deserve to know of my good fortune.

Chapter Two

THE INTERVIEW

Following an interview at Stratford Town Hall with Essex County Council Education Committee, who made up the board to select pupils for Elmbridge, Fyfield and Kennylands, I was offered a place at Fyfield.

I had gone to the Town Hall with just my Dad. The committee asked him lots of questions about my health and the school I was currently attending. He made it clear that whether or not I was offered a place at any of these schools, I was leaving my current school at the end of the term and probably being home-schooled due to his complete dissatisfaction with both the current school policies and the lack of education. He specifically complained that I was never chosen to do any sport because I was small for my age.

Then it was my turn, and they asked me what I most

liked about school, to which I replied that there wasn't anything I liked about school, but if they asked me what I disliked I would be able to come up with a very big list that we could talk about. They persisted with their inquisition and managed to extract that the only thing I had found useful about my current school was that I had learned to make apple crumble. Clearly they were not impressed. My Dad's face said it all. He was sure the interview was going badly.

Then one of the committee asked me what I most looked forward to should I be allocated a place. You couldn't shut me up, and even my Dad was a bit surprised that I could manage to speak more than one sentence.

So I was offered a place at Fyfield. We quickly accepted, and upon written confirmation we received a brochure about the school and an extensive clothing list. I had to go to a school outfitters called Henry Taylor's, in Hoe Street, Walthamstow, to get all the items. The shop was established in 1903 and is still there today.

The outing soon became a family affair, so my parents, brother, three grandparents and one of my aunts accompanied me to the shop. To be fair, the expense was being shared by all, so the event had to include them too.

I know my brother got a lot of enjoyment out of teasing me about all the items that needed to be purchased and fooled about holding each garment up to him, so I could see what it might look like. We all laughed so much it hurt!

To my ignorance and amusement, I had no idea what anyone used running spikes for, and no idea what hockey was, except that I needed this weird-shaped stick to play the game and even more weird boots to wear for that task, together with a very nice pair of long maroon pleated shorts to wear. I was reliably informed by the shop assistant that these were called 'games culottes'.

Before this shopping trip, I'd had no idea what most senior school games were. I lived in a city and we hadn't needed running spikes and hockey sticks in London, as little girls had no need of them. At my junior school all I had done in the way of sport was run around the gym and play indoor team games. We had played some ball games, climbed ropes and used the pommel horse and box. I did however belong to a very good gymnastics club, and was very good at all the disciplines.

I don't think I had ever been 'outside' for games. At the secondary modern we were all taken to the fields for sport, but I had sat on a bench watching a large number of my class smoke, and a select few play, as I was never chosen, being small. It was probably damage limitation on the school's part. The field was so far off in the distance that I never actually saw any games at all; I just waited for two hours until the coach came to take us back to school. So the prospect of actually playing some sport seemed quite exciting.

On top of this were purchased a long grey raincoat, socks, shirts, skirts, blazers, ties, summer dresses, cardigans, very thick grey regulation knickers, shorts, more sportswear and a school hat. Also 100 name tapes were ordered so that my Nan could put her sewing skills to the test before I finally left for school. I could have had green or blue name tabs, but despite green being my favourite colour, I went for blue so that it co-ordinated with the uniform, which was in the West Ham colours of blue and maroon.

We spent £102! The shop assistant looked exhausted. She said that we were a lovely family and it had been a real pleasure. In all it was a family afternoon out which lasted three hours, followed by tea at Nan's house afterwards.

To my absolute delight I was also allowed to go to the shoe shop and purchase three pairs of black shoes without ankle straps and buckles, which was a true sign of growing up. One pair of casual shoes was black patent. I danced around in those shoes for a whole week before they were packed.

For the very first time in my life I had a pair of slippers, a couple of pairs of black plimsolls and white plimsolls. I had never had the luxury of slippers at home, it was just bare feet. I'd never had white plimsolls to play tennis in before. One pair of the plimsolls was to be used as indoor shoes. I didn't actually understand this until I got to school and it was explained to me. I also had my first pair of hockey boots.

Apart from the uniform, other items were suggested that could be taken to school, but some were advised against. Games, books, sports equipment and musical instruments were in but dolls, teddy bears and photographs were out. Comics were also discouraged, which was a shame as I quite liked the Dandy, Beano and Diana. I also had a very large stash of 'banned' American comics that my Uncle George gave to me. He worked in Swiss Cottage as a piano tuner and had access to all sorts of American items. I expect it was via a customer. In the end I took a five-year diary, a pen, a long piece of elastic (for French skipping) and three tennis balls. I thought this would get me through my first term, until such time as I had to suss out what was really needed. By the time the second term came around I'd invested in some jacks with a small rubber ball, and more tennis balls. I had also taken back some of my own tuck and given strict instructions to grandparents about what was needed in future survival parcels. I stressed that as they were contributing money towards my time there, it would be a shame if I expired through lack of fruit cake before I had a chance to complete my studies. It worked!

I had only been to the countryside twice that I could remember; on a family holiday to the very exotic Isle of Sheppey, in Kent, where my Dad's mate had a wooden hut that we stayed at, and later in a caravan, but now I was off to the Essex countryside with the nearest town three miles away.

In preparation for boarding school, my parents gave me the *Observer's Book of British Trees*. I clearly remember being quite enamoured with 'Countryside and Seaside' and asked my Dad all sorts of questions about it on holiday. I think he was getting a bit fed up with the questions as I asked him why the dustbins had SBC (Sheppey Borough Council) written on them, and he said it stood for Sarah Bella Crayfish as they were her bins! I don't think I ever believed a word he said after that. Nobody could ever understand what a landscape meant to me, but perhaps it accounted for the fact that I had found an inner city park a wonderful and magical place.

Mum sat down with me one evening and talked to me about 'the birds and bees'. The next day Nan sat down with me and told me an awful lot more! This included several references to boys and having nothing to do with them - ever - to which I readily agreed, aged ten and a half. Having a younger brother, I wasn't actually that keen on boys anyway. All they did was tease you and play with your most interesting toys. My personal favourite toy was called the Magic Robot, which answered questions you asked it by pointing to the answer. Well, it did until my brother tested it out in the bath to see if it floated. He confirmed that it sank.

Dad bought a big second-hand travelling trunk, a big brown sturdy box which took all of my new wardrobe and chattels off to boarding school. In fact, I took everything I owned, except my lucky black pottery cat and my pressed flowers.

I had a special tea at church with all the rest of the choir members and promised I would go back to sing in the holidays too. Some of my customers cried when they thought I was going away, especially the little old lady who lived next door, but I had to promise to go in and see her as soon as I returned from school. A big group of people came and waved us off for that first journey to school. I wasn't sad and I wasn't nervous. I was bursting with happiness. I was now ready for my new life adventure.

Chapter Three

THE HISTORY OF FYFIELD
AND ITS DEVELOPMENT

The site of the school was at Clatterford End near the village of Fyfield. In 1857 the Industrial Schools Act was passed. The term 'Industrial School' was primarily used to house vagrant, destitute and disorderly children who were considered in danger of becoming criminals.

Certified industrial schools were promoted as an alternative to reformatories by a group of magistrates, MPs and social reformers under the Industrial Schools Act of 1857. Children aged seven to fifteen who were convicted of vagrancy could be placed in an Industrial School. A further Act in 1861 defined four categories of potential entrants: under-fourteens found begging; under-fourteens found wandering and homeless or frequenting with thieves; under-twelves who had committed an imprisonable offence; and under-fourteens whose parents could not control them.

From 1871, the children under fourteen of a woman twice convicted of 'crime' could be sent to an Industrial School. From 1880, any child under 14 found to be living in a brothel, or living with or associating with common or reputed prostitutes, could be sent to one.

For children who actually had committed criminal acts, Reformatory Schools were established.

The great majority of Industrial and Reformatory schools were privately operated, although subject to regular official inspection and licensing.

Truant School

On May 19 1885, the newly-constructed Victorian building on the Fyfield site opened as West Ham short-term Truant School for Boys. It cost £8000 to build.

The Truant School was another type of school that appeared following the 1870 and Amended 1876 Elementary Education Act. These were for children who persistently refused to attend elementary schools, and they could be detained for a period, typically of one to three months, under a very strict regime, and then released on a renewable licence to attend a conventional school.

In 1907 the school incorporated Industrial into its name so it was known as the West Ham Truant and Industrial School. It housed eighty children. It was re-certified on the 16th March 1912 for one hundred and ten children. It was described as a purpose-built premises with twenty acres of land. It closed in 1925.

I found some very interesting newspaper articles whilst researching the history of the School.

Extract from The London Gazette,
May 22 1885

Whitehall, May 20, 1885.
THE Secretary of State for the Home Department hereby gives notice, that the West Ham School Board Industrial Truant School, at Fyfield, Ongar, in the county of Essex, has been Certified by him as fit to be an Industrial School for the reception of Boys, not exceeding Eighty in number, under the provisions of 'The Industrial Schools Act, 1866.

Extract from a letter to
The Guardian, June 15 1898

The following Sunday those who went to chapel go to church, and those who went to church go to chapel. That is in a school for 150 Church of England children. In another they go to church in the morning and chapel in the evening. In another, they all go to chapel in the evening; and so on I might take a number of instances. In one the children are taken to church, but a section of them are taken by turns every Sunday—they are taken in rotation—to a Quakers' meeting. (Laughter.) In another, all go to church and chapel every Sunday, and in another, where they are nearly all Church of England children, they never go to church at all; they are taken to the Wesleyan chapel morning and evening, and I have here a letter from the vicar of the parish, who says that he has invited the children to attend the parish church of which I have the honour to be vicar. The managers will submit my offer to the committee - This was written some time ago - 'but I think it is little short of a scandal that our children should be taken away, and that they are not permitted to follow the faith of their parents and receive instruction in the religion of the Church.' I heard the other day from the same clergyman that his offer had been refused, and that all the Church of England children go to the Wesleyan chapel morning and evening. Well, then, with regard to the rule B of the school, and the cases in which these things are absolutely prohibited, in which the law is set aside, at the West Ham Industrial School the words of the Cowper - Triple clause are incorporated in the rules and quoted in inverted commas.

Extract from the London Gazette
11th October 1907

FYFIELD CERTIFIED INDUSTRIAL AND TRUANT SCHOOL.

The Secretary of State for the Home Department hereby gives notice that he has this day granted a new Certificate to the School heretofore known as the West Ham Truant Industrial School at Fyfield, with a view to the admission into the said School of such boys as may be sent thereto from time to time in pursuance of the Industrial -Schools Act, 1866 (29 and 30 Vic.,cap. 118), and of the Acts amending the same, or under the Elementary Education Act, 1876 (39 and 40 Vic., cap. 79).The School will be known as the 'Fyfield Certified Industrial and Truant School.' The Certificate authorizes the reception into the School of 80 boys. Whitehall, 10th October, 1907. (The London Gazette, 1907)

Residential Open Air School

By April 1925 the dual-purpose Industrial and Truant School was redesignated as 'West Ham Residential Open Air School for Delicate Children'. It housed 80 boys. It was enlarged during 1931 to accept 60 girls as well. The school had a considerable collection of buildings. The main block was two to three storeys high made of brick with red-brick dressings. It remained an Open Air School until 1956, when it was no longer considered necessary to have this special category of school for children. Many of the children were sent to the open air school to avoid them getting tuberculosis, popularly known as consumption. During the 1920s, tuberculosis was one of Britain's most urgent health problems, especially in the East End of London, because Britain was quickly becoming industrialized. It was not until after World War II that BCG vaccine received widespread acceptance in Britain. This probably explains why there was less need for an Open Air School after 1956.

After 1956, the premises were taken over as a residential school by Essex County Council. Mr Smith had been headmaster of the Open Air School until 1953, when the Deputy Head Mr Underwood took over. Mr Underwood subsequently moved to another job when the school closed in 1956. However, Mr Underwood was persuaded to return in order to open Fyfield County Boarding School in 1958.

Fyfield County Boarding School

In the beginning, the co-educational boarding school had around eighty-five pupils. There were many further buildings erected during the 1960s with Newham (North East West Ham) or Derwent dormitory being the first, followed by a Sick Bay, Common Room and further dormitories named Churchill, Kings and Queens, in addition to the existing dormitories of Trinity, Merton, Clare and Sommerville.

A teaching block was also built during 1962. Pupil numbers began to grow, and when I was there in 1965, there were 234 pupils on the School Roll.

In all around 1200 children were educated at Fyfield County Boarding School from 1958 until 1980. This averaged an intake of around 36 pupils a year.

I understand that further buildings were completed during the 1970s. Following this Fyfield Boarding School merged with Kennylands School and relocated and reopened as Hockerill School at Bishops Stortford during 1980. It attained Grant Maintained status in 1995 and later during 1998 became known as Hockerill Anglo-European College, when it gained music college status.

There were also changes to the name when the old Fyfield site was renamed and became Elmbridge School in 1980. Elmbridge School physically relocated to the site from Cranleigh, Surrey. During the 1990s it closed when the site was acquired for redevelopment as a housing site.

The Victorian part of the school became a listed building.

DESCRIPTION: Elmbridge School

GRADE: II

DATE LISTED: 29 June 1984

ENGLISH HERITAGE BUILDING ID: 118369

OS GRID REFERENCE: TL5626406246

OS GRID COORDINATES: 556264, 206246

LATITUDE/LONGITUDE: 51.7331, 0.2615

The site was then sold on for development around 1995 and was named Elmbridge Hall in 2000. The Victorian buildings have now been converted into 18 housing units and an estate of 34 new houses constructed.

During 2011 I was busy trying to find some history about the school when I stumbled upon some very interesting exchanges of email between pupils that went to the School between the World War II and the mid-1950s. It seems that things were not that different, except that they spent a lot of time outdoors or resting on camp beds in the open air and doing lots of lessons outdoors too. I learnt that their dormitories were called Fyfield, Moreton and Roding and were also exposed to the elements.

School Houses

Our house names were taking from the Rodings, or Roothings as they were called many years ago. The Rodings were the largest group of villages to have a common name. It is thought that during the sixth century Hroða sailed up the Thames and into a little tributary to settle. The river and the villages derived their name from him. The villages were in the Dunmow Hundred in the time of Edward the Confessor and recorded in the Domesday Book.

The villages were almost inaccessible and remained that way for centuries. There were no buildings of any importance until much later.

So the names of our houses at Fyfield were named after the Anglo Saxon community known as the Hroðingas.

Abbess – Purple

The Roding is thought to be named after the Eleanor, Abbess of Barking, as it was called Roding Abatesse in 1237, although it was called Berwic Roding prior to this. A Roman Road divides the parish in two, with a manor house and a church. The house was named Rockwood. It is thought that Elizabeth I visited it and discussed the Plague there with her privy council. John Thurloe, a noted famous person, who was the son of the rector, was in Government under Cromwell, and also came from Abbess Roding. His portrait is in the National Gallery.

Aythorpe – Blue

In medieval times the Lord of Aythorpe, Henry Bouchier, was beheaded for declaring Jane Grey Queen and Anne, his daughter, succeeded, although Elizabeth I declared Anne's heirs illegitimate.

The area has a medieval building and a public house called the Axe and Compasses, where stage coaches used to call on their route into London. It apparently used to have many windmills, but now in the twenty-first century there is only one left. The post mill is the largest in Essex. It has a hook for hauling up boiling water, still in place near to the fireplace. It also has a thirteenth-century church.

It is rumoured that in Aythorpe Roding in 1652 a woman called Mrs Day died from spontaneous combustion. It seems it was all happening in Aythorpe!

Beauchamp - Green

Not that much remains of Beauchamp Roding - a bit like our old school really. It is really only field and there isn't anything of much significance associated with the Roding. That is not to say that there was never anything there, but history does not really tell us anything about it. It was held by the Earl of Bretagne during the time of the Domesday Book.

There is however a parish church called St Botolph in Beauchamp Roding which stands on a hill in the vicinity of woods and a meadow, completely isolated. There may have been a Saxon church at the same site, some time before the present 14th century one. You have to drive up a muddy track to it from the main road north of Fyfield. There is a large glacial rock which is not from the area placed in the churchyard, known as the Beauchamp Roding Puddingstone. It might be megalithic, as the hill position and the dedication to a Saxon Abbot might lend some credence to this as early Christians tended to re-use pagan sites but nobody knows for sure.

Berners Roding - Yellow

Following Uluric, who was the last of the Saxon Lords, the Roding was given to Hugh De Berners as a reward for fighting in William the Conqueror's army. Once again it is recorded in the Domesday Book.

Juliana Berners was famous for hunting and hawking and her poetry is in the book of St Albans, which is one of the earliest works printed in English. The Berners family remained loyal to the Monarchy.

So which house was the best during my leaving year? Today, over forty years on, it is still debated. We still have a bit of banter about it, even recently when collecting donations for the clock restoration. As reported by the House Officials, here are the extracts from the very first edition of the Fyfield School Magazine 1969-1970 (School Magazine, produced solely by the pupils).

Abbess - So far this year Abbess have not done articularly well in most of the inter house competitions. (JM)

Berners - This year Berners has not really shown their ability to the School. (CW)

Beauchamp - Firstly, our successes. (ND)

Aythorpe - Aythorpe had quite a good year's activity. (RW)

I expect you have guessed correctly which House I was in - Beauchamp. Not that I am in anyway sore that we came second to Berners in the clock restoration appeal!

Since the final closure of the school site and the construction of attractive modern accommodation there, I was very interested to read that the old Victorian building, which still stands, has spy holes within its structure. Surveillance was an important means of controlling behaviour in Victorian times and a number of the observation portals have survived. When I was at Fyfield there used to be spooky stories that scared us all, about a resident ghost and a bell that rang of its own accord. These stories had no evidence to back them up, but they were traditionally passed down the generations of school pupils.

Some ex-pupils gave a donation to the current residents so that they could get the clock tower fixed. It was reported in the Brentwood Gazette in 2013 that 'The alumni of Fyfield Boarding School raised over £1000 for their former school's clock tower to be repaired'. The residents have put a plaque in the Victorian building to identify the previous users of the building. This sparked some debate as to whether the wording is entirely correct, as in my time at the school it was never, as I recall, referred to as a Secondary Modern School. Nor did it operate along the lines of a Secondary Modern School. However, the previous status of the school really doesn't matter that much. We thought it was a really good thing that the residents did this, to record and preserve the history of the site.

The plaque reads:

West Ham Truant Industrial School 1884
Fyfield Certified Truant and Industrial School 1907
West Ham Open Air Residential School 1925
Fyfield Secondary Modern Boarding School 1958
Elmbridge School 1980
Elmbridge Hall 2000

I checked with Ofsted, knowing that there had been some discussion as to what the school was called during our time there, and the school after 1958 was never referred to as a Secondary Modern School. Its official title was Fyfield County Secondary Boarding School in all the inspection documents after Mr Perry became Headmaster, and prior to that, when Mr Underwood was Headmaster, it was just Fyfield County Boarding School. They were described as maintained schools until 1978.

Hansard, May 25 1978, written answers (Commons), Education and Science:

<u>Mr Christopher Price</u> asked the Secretary of State for Education and Science to list in the Official Report (a) the maintained boarding schools and units, respectively, in England and Wales, (b) those of these boarding schools and units which have already gone comprehensive, (c) those concerning which plans for reorganisation are outstanding, and (d) those for which no plans are outstanding.

<u>Miss Margaret Jackson</u>

The information requested is as follows:

Maintained Boarding Schools and schools with Boarding Units for which proposals have been received or approved under section 13 of the Education Act 1944 to implement comprehensive reorganization.

Boarding Schools
Essex:
• Fyfield School.
• Elmbridge School (Boarding at Cranleigh).
• Kennyland School.

I'm not sure it is very important to categorise what it was called, but more important to describe what it was like. Having previously attended a Secondary Modern, I am sure it was not run along the same lines. I met a few pupils that had passed the 11+ in my time there. There was a very wide range of subjects taught as well as a wide range of ability too.

Sources:

The Guardian (1885, June 15), London, London, UK. Retrieved July 28th, 2013

The London Gazette (1907, 10 11), London.

The London Gazette (1885), The London Gazette. London, UK. Retrieved 07 28, 2013

HANSARD 1803-2005 → 1970s → 1978 → May 1978 → 25 May 1978 → Written Answers (Commons) → EDUCATION AND SCIENCE

Chapter Four

REMEMBERING THE 1960S

Let me try to paint you a picture of the 1960s. When I try to think back, what usually come to my mind are events that are associated with the time. For instance a friend of mine put a photograph onto a social networking site with a caption 'remember the time we queued for tickets to see the Beatles outside the Granada Walthamstow', and sure enough there we were in that queue. At the time of the new pop music era, our parents had said we were wasting our money and that the Beatles would never last. This was just before I went to Fyfield.

The world was changing. The years from 1960 through to 1969 were later referred to as the 'swinging sixties'. It was the decade which signalled the birth of pop music and with that went a change in fashion and behaviour too.

This is what I can remember of the 1960s as a teenager.

As I started with a music event, I will continue with that. Pop was the first choice of most people who were young in the 60s. Our favourites were the Beatles, the Rolling Stones, Elvis Presley, the Yardbirds, the Kinks, the Who and Cream during the earlier years at school. The later years at Fyfield my taste in music had changed and Jimi Hendrix, Led Zeppelin, the Troggs and Bob Dylan were what I listened to. I'm not even sure I liked them all, but it seemed trendy at the time.

A whole new range of music had developed, and with that emerged sub-cultures, the Mods, who often wore suits and rode scooters, and the Rockers, who wore leather jackets and rode heavy motorbikes. Musically there was not much common ground. Rockers were into Elvis and, as their name suggests, Rock music and the Mods favoured Ska, like the Who. My Dad had Norton Villiers and BSA motorbikes, so you might guess who influenced me most. I still admire bikes. I returned to Walthamstow during June 2014, primarily to take some photographs for this book and I was very pleased to see a bike behind the front wall of the old house that I used to live in. My Dad would have approved.

Later as I was leaving school, two new cultures were developing, hippies and skinheads. Mods and Rockers were fading fast. The older generation preferred Cliff Richard and the Shadows, Gerry and the Pacemakers, the Searchers and Herman's Hermits. As my Nan said 'such nice boys, with catchy tunes'. We were not of the age to appreciate nice boys with catchy tunes. Far from it!

Transistor radios had become really popular during the sixties. Millions had been manufactured and they were affordable too. Although they had been developed earlier, they had been miniaturised by this time and so were portable, being pocket-sized. They enabled us to listen to pirate radio stations, such as Radio Caroline, the first British pirate radio station, which started broadcasting from a ship off the Essex coast in 1964. Radio London, Radio Luxembourg and Invicta were also popular stations. However most of these were curtailed by legislation and new BBC radio stations were established in 1967 with Radio 1 being the pop station. The first song played by Tony Blackburn was on a Saturday at 7 am and was Flowers in the Rain by the Move, so at least it was rock! The music on Radio 1 was censored and some of our favourites were not played as often as we would have liked. It was somewhere musically between the young generation and my Nan's, depending on the programme. However it was one step on from 'Sing Something Simple' and 'Billy Cotton's Band Show'. The time when I most listened to the radio was when I got up in the morning before breakfast. Somehow it enticed you to get out of bed. Sometimes we were awake and just waiting until we could switch the radio on. This programme went by the captivating name of Daily Disk Delivery. We called it the Tony Blackburn show. Although we all had radios, only one per dormitory was allowed as the 'official' radio. We used to choose the one that would operate the loudest.

The sixties was a time when teenagers could express

themselves. It was a time when everything was changing after the dismal post-war fifties. The East End of London was almost as dismal as you could get. It was poverty.

Football was another feature of the sixties. A season ticket to what is now called a Premier Division club cost around £8.50 for the season. England hosted the World Cup (and won it!) but as girls didn't watch football much, we only got to see a bit of it. I cannot remember where we watched, but it was in the private accommodation of one of the teachers - possibly Matron's. Geoff Hurst and Martin Peters were much talked about from that moment on at Fyfield. It was our introduction to football and we loved it.

Television was not widely available at school. In the later years we did have a television room. Programmes that were shown were not really the sort that would entice a teenager to view such as 'Emergency Ward 10', the quiz show 'Double Your Money', 'Opportunity Knocks', 'Sunday Night at the London Palladium', 'Dixon of Dock Green' and 'The Adventures of Robin Hood'. Most of them in the early days were after our bedtime, or broadcast at times when we had better things to do.

By the mid-sixties television was developing. I remember not being interested at all, although the exception of this was 'Juke Box Jury' in the early days, mainly to hear the panellist Janice Nicholls say 'Oi'll give it foive' in her Birmingham accent, which used to make us laugh, mainly because she used to say it for nearly every record. Top of the Pops (7.30 pm Thursday) had always been popular, as was The Saint. During our fourth and fifth years at Fyfield, the house that had won the house point shield for that week got to watch 'Top of the Pops', but it soon developed into a much wider group. I also enjoyed being scared by 'Dr Who', and quickly became a fan. Oddly enough we used to tell the little ones at school that it was all true, and they got so scared that they left the room.

When occasionally I stayed with Nan in the holidays, she watched 'Coronation Street', 'The Black and White Minstrel Show', 'Z Cars' and 'Dr Finlay's Casebook'. 'Peyton Place' too was a very big drama of the sixties and seemed to be on the television forever! My parents had not been that keen on television during the early years, so my viewing was limited both at home and school. I never missed television and regarded it as a 'big occasion' instrument, something special, but not as an everyday activity. It really didn't hold my interest.

Anyway living in London meant that there were always others things to do, such as bonfire night, outdoor swimming, singing, concerts and visiting relatives. Socialising was and is still big in London. It was traditional to go to someone house to play cards, play the piano, sing, drink, and smoke and generally have a good time. This happened every Saturday night, and it was amazing, as you would have thought we hadn't seen each other for ages. It was so noisy. We also had a break at half-time, which was generally between 9.30 and 10 pm, where we all sat down for supper of cold ham, salad, bread and pickles. The children were also allowed a chocolate milkshake called Mickey that my granddad used to bring home and occasionally ice cream, but there was also birthday cake too and it always seemed as if it was someone's birthday.

My brother Jeff, being the youngest, had always fallen asleep by this time, but I got wise to missing the supper very early on and had an afternoon nap, so I could stay the course. I got the hang of smoking before I was five and could roll a cigarette and had the taste for gin and orange, which was their fault for leaving it in their glasses for so long. Whenever I got caught with either, it was 'Oh bless, she is so sweet'. I really looked at that age very sweet. Health concerns around smoking and drinking were pretty much non-existent.

The next big sixties event was following the first man into space, and television was to screen a man walking on the Moon - in colour. I did witness this event on television, on a set that was set up in Kings dormitory boot room for us to see. It was not colour though, as this was a pretty new invention and was costly. ITV and BBC1 were first shown in colour in 1969. I was really amazed by colour TV. It was such a talking point.

We also saw the Prince of Wales' investiture on television, although to us, it was not quite as wonderful as seeing a manned space flight and a landing on the Moon. I don't think I really understood why or what an investiture was. It didn't capture my imagination. The only bit that registered was that he would probably one day be King.

Looking back there were many memorable events during the sixties, some before I went to Fyfield, such as Martin Luther King's 'I have a dream' speech, and I knew quite a lot about this because my grandmother's brother, Ernie, had given an oil painting which he had painted to Martin Luther King and it had been the talk within the family for some time.

The death of President John F Kennedy was talked about by my family and others for weeks, but it never meant a lot to me because I don't think I really understood who he was at the time.

Princess Margaret's wedding in 1960 was the first television programme I remember seeing, sitting around someone's TV with all my aunties - there were such a lot of them!

The Profumo affair, in which a Government Minister was forced to resign over an affair with a prostitute, was a scandal that everyone was gossiping about, but not in front of their children.

There were shops which were between a supermarket and a corner shop, one of which was Sainsbury's, a big grocery store with ceramic tiles around the shop and a stone floor, which gave it an air of cleanliness. We had bacon, sliced thick, medium or thin. All the shop assistants wore turbans around their hair. It all looked hygienic.

However, before this we shopped just at corner shops - even in the East End of London. The first supermarkets were opening, although I had never been to one during the sixties. In my errand running scheme I remember the horror of bread going up to one shilling and threepence, which equates to about just over 6p in today's money. I remember my Dad saying to me 'Well, with inflation during your lifetime, bread will probably reach £1 a loaf'. I thought at the time he was totally mad and I remember my Mum saying that she wished he didn't say these ridiculous things, but what could you do? Sliced bread was introduced and we all went mad for it. Not only did we eat the bread, but we used the waxed paper it was wrapped in for all sorts, such as school lunch and picnics. My Mum washed it and hung it on the line to dry! Some of it lined our boots in winter, so our socks didn't get wet.

Some people were lucky enough to have a twin-tub washing machine, but ordinary people like my family had only the boiler and a wringer and then a spin dryer. During the sixties a launderette opened near to us and we had a Friday evening out to the launderette, where I think it cost us around two shillings to wash the clothes and sixpence to tumble dry them. Up till then we had sent the sheets and big items to a laundry collection service in a green bag and they were returned the next week, ready to use. The launderette trip was progress and was a family event and a good night out, especially as Dad bought us a bag of chips to eat whilst we waited for the laundry.

Later during my time at school, in 1967, the sinking of the *Torrey Canyon*, a ship which carried crude oil and went down in Cornwall, was a disaster which was much reported and talked about.

In preparation for decimalisation our mathematics teacher explained to us the principles of the new money, although to be fair we didn't really know whether or not this was going to actually happen, as the Government hadn't made up its mind at that time. We thought we would never be able to cope with it, and as some older people said, if they had known we were going to be decimalised they would have learnt to count beyond 21. There was no use in learning above and beyond a guinea, or 21 shillings.

Another big issue of the sixties was Dr Beeching's pruning of under-used railways. This was discussed a lot, as some of my family either worked for the railways or used trains frequently. Trains ran on coal and steam, later to be replaced by electricity. I remember going for a day out to Southend or Canvey Island by steam train. The train went to Southend, or we used to get off at South Benfleet station and take a bus to Canvey Island.

Electricity was now in most homes, but a few of my family and Jewish friends still had gas mantels. I used to light many of these with a taper for my customers, especially on Friday evenings. The reason was that most of my customers were elderly, so sometimes they used to leave the gas on without remembering to light it, and my Jewish customers could not and did not light them after daylight on Fridays. I had a childhood obsession about checking that the gas was off, until at some point we changed over to North Sea gas, which couldn't kill you. Well, not quite as easily. My Nan was very nervous about turning on the electricity, in case it went bang. She thought it might leak out of the wires and kill her. It took us quite a while to convince her that it was safe to use, and then when she got the hang of it, she got every gadget possible, but the best was a fridge with a freezer box inside, instead of the pantry.

She had a habit of being swanky with her friends, asking them if they fancied an ice cream and wafer. She had a real liking for Neapolitan ice cream, fortunately.

Where I lived in Walthamstow later became known as part of Waltham Forest, and tower blocks of flats started to be built everywhere. My Nan and Granddad moved into one of them after their lovely little terraced house was compulsorily purchased. I had been very proud of my Nan for protesting and standing firm right up until eviction day, but after several reprieves she was eventually evicted.

Their new flat had underfloor heating, a lift that never seemed to work and extensive views of other buildings across London. It was meant to be a solution to the housing shortage that had been caused by the last war, mainly because London had been bombed and people were still living in prefabs, and we were now seeing a population increase commonly referred to as the Baby Boom. It was a shame that the council officials and developers failed on two accounts, firstly to properly recompense them so they could actually buy another property, and secondly not to have the common sense to provide accommodation, so that my Granddad, who was very ill, could actually go outside. The authorities had taken full advantage by evicting a woman and her very ill husband. My Nan often phoned Social Services and invited them round to discuss the problem.

Nan and Granddad remained on the 7th floor, until Social Services and the medical profession had just about had enough of visiting them by walking up 14 flights of stairs on a daily basis, when it was decided that they should be rehoused in a ground floor property with a suitable outside space. However, it was too late by then and Granddad died within six months of moving to a pleasant location, with a shared garden. My Nan then found fame in the local press, because the council wanted to rehouse her again in a smaller one-person high-rise property and she complained that they were harassing her after bereavement. She stayed in mourning for three years, wearing black and getting her photograph in the paper. A lot of people took her side, and eventually the council backed down. They wanted her to have only a single bedroom, and in her flat she had a double bedroom, which they said was too big. Fifty years on and the Government are still obsessed by bedrooms! My Nan, a lifelong Labour supporter, changed allegiance, just as a short-term protest.

During this time my Dad built us an indoor bathroom. The outside toilet became an inside one and a wash-basin and bath were installed. Gone were the tin baths in front of the sitting room fire. This was progress.

I am glad I lived through this era, as it was such a period of change.

Chapter Five

SCHOOL LIFE

I quickly had to adapt to a very new set of routines at boarding school. The main difference was that everyone did the same, so it was easy to follow.

Before going to boarding school I had been in charge of myself. This meant that I heard my parents get up, so knew I had to. I got myself washed and dressed, I got myself breakfast; I washed up my breakfast things, I got myself off for the two-mile walk to school. I had to be sensible crossing two busy roads in London. I got myself home at lunchtime (called dinner time in London), I got myself back to school for the afternoon and home again after school. We didn't have a uniform, as nobody could afford one. Mostly I wore second-hand clothes that were at least two sizes too big and had previously belonged to a girl called Kaye, the daughter of my Nan's friend. I was grateful though, because some of them were very pretty and I knew they would last for a while too. But it was so nice to be wearing exactly the same as everyone else.

At boarding school the day started when we got up at 7.30 in time to get washed and dressed in time to get to breakfast by 8.00. Most of us got there on time. There were only ever a couple of girls who were late, and if they had a reasonable excuse then nothing was done. If you were very late and didn't have a credible excuse, then a small punishment followed, but this really depended on which teacher was on duty. There were a couple of very understanding teachers who just accepted that sometimes people were late, but the one thing you never knew was just who it would be on duty. Every teacher went easy on anyone new.

Following breakfast there was a period where you went back to the dormitory to sweep the floor and made sure that your bed was made correctly, that the place was tidy and that you had everything you needed for the day. The Post Monitors collected the mail from the school office to distribute to their respective dormitories. There was very little time to read any letters, which usually had to wait until the first break or a quick peek at assembly. I always liked a letter from my Nan as she would have Sellotaped a shilling to it. I also loved being the Post Monitor, as there was an element of excitement to going to the School Office to collect mail. It was also lovely to know that the power of distributing mail made you popular.

We had a dormitory inspection when our bed was looked at, and if you had missed your 'hospital corners' or your pink counterpane was uneven, you were instructed to remake it.

This rarely happened after the first couple of months, because by then we were in the swing of it. We had also mastered the art of co-operation by helping each other to get the covers on correctly. The area under the bed was examined for dust, and whoever was on sweeping duty would have to sweep it again if it had not been done properly. About once a term we also had a drawer inspection, where everything had to be folded neatly. This took hours to get right. One girl was so good; she was always aiming for perfection, so we used to mess up her drawer so she was in the same boat as the rest of us. I remember feeling a tad guilty when she cried, but not for long!

Less attention was paid the older we became, as we had really become responsible enough to make sure everything was as it should be, as it saved time. To be honest we kept the drawer tidy and all our untidy stuff was put into our end-of-term trunks, as they were kept in our dormitory during the last year, whereas in earlier years they were taken to storage. Whoever was in charge hadn't quite got the measure of our antics.

We stood for assembly when we were young, but at some point it became a seated affair, possibly after the drugget was introduced, as we had to walk from the classroom with our chairs, then later from the dining room across to the hall and back again after it finished. This must have kept Matron busy, as often the chairs were weapons of mass leg destruction. Perhaps it was that girls just hadn't mastered walking quick enough in front of boys.

Prefects took it in turn to read lessons; some stories had a moral of a semi-religious nature and others were of a more general nature, such as the seasons, or a poem. From what I recall it was the personal choice of the prefect. There was always piano-playing by one of the teachers or an advanced piano student, for about five minutes or so until everyone was seated. My favourite piece was played by a male teacher who had a lovely light touch on the keys; it was 'In a Monastery Garden'. There was a prayer and a hymn, followed by a roundup of sports results and, important reminders. Once a week the house point trophy was awarded, when a coloured ribbon was tied on before it was re-hung on the wall. This was the start of our school day and week.

The summer and winter timetables differed in that during the winter we had afternoon free time and evening lessons, whilst in the summer lessons continued through the day and then we had free time. However, mostly we had prep after supper. I can only remember a few times when the day was so wonderful weather-wise that the Headmaster said prep was cancelled and we were to spend the time on the field. Some of that time was just idled away making daisy chains and chatting.

Prep was staggered for each year, with the youngest going to bed first and subsequent years following. There was usually prep, a half-hour of free time and then wash and bed, with lights out starting at 7.30 for the first year, then at half-hour intervals for each year, with prefects being allowed coffee at 9 pm and bed at around 10 pm, because they were very often supervising getting the lower years to bed.

The house that won the house points trophy for the week was allowed to go to the television room to watch Top of the Pops. I don't really remembering watching very much television at school at all. However we often did win the House points trophy in my last year of school and I don't think a week went past when I didn't watch Top of the Pops. Part of the programme was about music, but it was also about fashion too, what hairstyles they had, what they were wearing and how they danced. It was also about drooling over your favourite group, those groups that our parents told us wouldn't last.

Obviously too the school day was structured around activities that required light, so games were generally before lunch during the winter. During winter afternoons we were allowed free time before tea, but it always felt strange to me that we were in class during cold winter evenings when it was dark. This was 4.30 to 6.30. I vividly remember the crunch of frost under your feet and the smell of the damp evening air when coming out of prep during the last year I was at school. Despite the weather we didn't wear our coats.

During the summer months we were in school until 16.00, had tea and then were free until 6.30.

We did however do lots of activities during free time. I don't remember anyone ever complaining that they were bored. You could go swimming, go out for a walk, go to the village shop, team sports, reading, extra art class, needlework or private study and the younger pupils were allowed to just play. You could listen to music or practise your instrument. You could also phone home if you wanted to, from the pay box in the quadrangle. When I went into the fourth year a tuck shop was opened within the school too, and this proved to be popular. In the fifth year we were allowed to go and wash our hair during free time too. The only thing you were not allowed to do was be idle and cause mischief.

Saturdays and Sundays were different, with a lot of free time on Saturday, after prep finished at 11.30 until the school dance for the top two forms or evening film, which was compulsory in all but the fifth year. Sunday was similar, it was church or prep, the choice was yours. There was a school service at 4pm on a Sunday, then high tea and after that was compulsory letter-writing home.

Although this was a usual routine, it was also full of one-off activities, concerts, trips out, weekend's home and school functions, such as open day, fete day, speech day, drama events etc when the school had visitors.

Before bed we had locker inspection after shoe cleaning. Well, some did. I don't remember it being so in the last year. I also learnt that the fewer shoes you had the less trouble you would get into, so those with four or more pair of shoes had more cleaning than the rest of us. I also learnt that treading in puddles when you came off the hockey pitch reduced the amount of boot cleaning.

The whole of school life was about routine, and once you had learnt it, it was easy. It always felt busy.

The history of the House system, school council and assemblies

There were four houses during the years 1965-1970. These were Abbess, Aythorpe, Beauchamp and Berners. They were named after Anglo Saxon villages known as the Rodings of North Essex. I was in Beauchamp, the green house. Not a popular house, as there was scary stories about the green ghost, but I was happy. Green is my favourite colour.

The Abbess colour was mauve, Aythorpe was blue and Berners was yellow. Each new intake of pupils was split into groups for a house. Various inter-house competitions took place, where a ribbon or a cup was won and points were given towards the Cock House Cup.

There were various competitions such as an inter-house drama festival, music and a speech competition, senior and junior football, netball, softball and rounders, cricket and hockey competitions, a table tennis event and a cross country event, to name but a few. There were also points to be won for swimming and athletics too.

I took part in the speech competition, not because I was a good speaker, but because I did want to improve, and anyone could just speak. No special skill needed there. My English teacher helped me to improve considerably throughout the time I was at school; she listened to me and corrected me. Not only that, but she gave me a lot of confidence. My favourite new word quickly became 'lugubrious', from a poem by John Blight, 'Death of a Whale'. I remember going through school with favourite words. Every term there were new ones. My parents used to say, 'Where does she get them from?' as if they were collectors' items.

The house points shield was given every week, and during 1970 Beauchamp won it most weeks, to the other houses' annoyance. This also meant that Beauchamp took the 'Cock House Cup' that year, 1970.

Traditionally, the school had a Head Boy and Head Girl and each house had two prefects who were called House Officials. There were some additional posts, such as catering official, Secretary to the School Council and Head Librarian. There were also some extra prefects without any specific role in duties. This made up what was known as the School Council. I was the Head Librarian, which was not really surprising, as my main pastime was reading and I could usually be found in the school library. This just made my book reading seem official, rather than casual.

At our first meeting of the council in the September of 1969, all the tasks of the council were divided up. One of the main topics at council meetings was always food, because it was difficult for all the pupils to be happy with all of the food all the time. The first decision the council made was to try having an optional tea at 4 pm, every day apart from Sunday. It was noted at the first meeting, though that the school was satisfied with the standard of school food.

It was also decided that the winner of the House points system was to be rewarded by being allowed to watch 'Top of the Pops', or be able to sign out during Saturday morning prep time. You were allowed to do both, but when you had exams looming it was not that practical to sign out on a Saturday. No wonder all those Beauchamp House pupils became so musically gifted, as we watched 'Top of the Pops' most Thursday evenings.

The council were concerned that there were some pupils

who were letting their houses down and not having any punishment for losing house points. I'm not exactly sure how any one person could lose up to five points a day, as things generally were pretty lenient, but some did, ending the week with a loss of 45 points! There were some repeat offenders. The outcome was to alter the system so that the house suffered less than the individual. Those losing more than five points were to be punished, and each house was to be credited with five points per pupil. This was agreed by all. It made it very good for my House, as we generally had a whole good bunch of non-losers and about three who had significant losses each week.

At our House meeting we devised a strategy to help those who lost a lot of House points to improve; we mentored the persistent offenders in turns throughout every day. It seemed worth it, and it worked too. In turn those offenders learned the routines very quickly and started to improve as well. It was a win-win situation. Also in the sports, the people who were good mentored those who wanted to improve, and we had a bit of luck there too. I suppose I was part of a very forward-thinking house.

In the spring term the Council discussed the need to increase the number of dances and reported an improvement in the organisation of them. This was because new school staff had helped the whole of the fifth form to arrange them better, and also the hall had on occasion been decorated, which gave a much more inviting feel to the evening. It was also decided that at certain times of the year, such as Halloween, Christmas and at the school leavers' dance, there would be a fully-decorated hall. The decorations were magnificent and took about 25 pupils all the afternoon to fully decorate. The school leavers' dance was traditionally attended by all staff as well as pupils, with the younger pupils leaving early. The favourite finishing song during 1969-70 was 'Hey Jude', mainly because it was the longest, lasting around five minutes. I felt lucky that I was always asked by someone for the last dance and not left there just watching. Anything to have a long last dance and a slightly later bedtime!

During the 1970 summer term, things moved on in the council meetings, with one chap having regular outbursts about individual pupils and another wandering away from the discussions. The boys were concerned that the girls were not giving enough input to meetings, whereas they were probably just politely listening to the boys, or maybe bored. I think hormones had quite a bit to do with the assertiveness of the boys, or what my mother might have termed 'showing off'. We did though have a couple of very eccentric personalities, otherwise referred to as 'characters' on the School Council, who used to regularly make us laugh, and eventually we all learnt to get along. I don't remember many other years having such a diverse and interesting, indeed slightly eccentric, array of personalities.

Prior to leaving, the School Council had a formal dinner with some of the staff in the staff room. It was traditional to dress up. For the girls it was often the first time they had worn a long evening dress. I bought myself a very cheap dress from a second-hand shop and altered it beyond recognition. It had pale green stripes. I trimmed it with matching flowers, with a low neck, and I had to wear my biggest platform shoes so that it did not trail on the ground when I walked. I left the bust measurement at 36 inches, altered the waist to 19 inches and fortunately the hips were already 36 inches. Despite being useless at needlework, I was keen to look nice at the dinner.

All the girls spent a long time creating unusual hairstyles, putting on make-up and painting their nails, whereas the boys put on clean shirts and casual suits. However one of our male prefects did wear a bow tie, which led to a lot of discussion. None of us had ever been to dinner before and it was part of our education. Most of the conversation that evening revolved around what we wanted to do after we left school. I remember it finished at 11 pm. It was held in the staff dining room, and when we walked back the air was beautifully scented by newly-cut grass.

In 1970 an opinion poll of the fourth and fifth formers was organised for the first time. It covered a whole range of questions, but some of the results were surprising: 93% were glad that they were being educated at a co-educational school, 59% were against having any more free time, 65% liked, and said they attended, school dances, 61% said they liked the countryside location of Fyfield, 77% welcomed sex education and, not so surprising, 61% were against have a formal school assembly. School assemblies changed so that all pupils were seated and the assembly covered a lot more than hymn singing and prayers. Most of the school notices were given at assembly, whereas previously they had been given after meals had finished.

The only real way to get out of going to assembly was to go to see Matron in Sick Bay. A lot of pupils did this regularly, as she ran her verruca clinic first every morning. It seems strange to think that having a verruca was preferable to attending assembly! Religion in our school wasn't so much about beliefs; it was about conforming to what was considered socially acceptable behaviour and approved of by parents. Only half of mine approved. My Dad said he thought that it would be better if I had spent the time doing something far more constructive, like learning how to de-coke the engine of a motorbike. My mother said it was far more useful to help Matron than sing hymns. So for the majority of the time I was with Matron, who said she liked having me there because I was cheerful and pleasant. Basically this amounted to making tea and biscuits for her and the doctor. My other job was to send people into her surgery in turn. I used to get rid of the boys first, as the doctor was always a little bit enthusiastic at the beginning of the verruca session, which was once a week. Also I never fainted or felt unwell at the sight of blood or vomit.

At one assembly the Headmaster was very annoyed about the names appearing on the fifth form girls' laundry lists. We had a rather unfortunate policy of dirty laundry having to be checked by another girl, to ensure it was really dirty and needed to be laundered before despatch on a Friday to the laundry. It was the whole indignity of someone checking that your underwear both smelt and was dirty that I rebelled against. Laundry was a service done by an off-site service provider, who had complained that the list of clothes to be laundered was often inaccurate. The 'new' Headmaster asked various girls to stand on their chairs at assembly and report how certain famous actors and pop stars had in fact signed the girl's laundry lists and asked what they were doing in a girls' dormitory. As I recall, we were slightly less worried about explaining ourselves than the fact that the fifth form boys had a very good view of our underwear whilst we were standing on the chair. This turned into the funniest spectacle as the rest of the school were laughing, then the teachers found it hard to suppress their laughter too. Three girls fell off their chairs, and the Headmaster was becoming less tolerant by the minute. He was the only person not to see this as something hilarious, and because hardly anybody took him seriously, he became more and more angry. He was a fairly easy-going chap, mostly, but this had annoyed him. The angrier he became the more we all laughed, until he marched furiously from the room. Finally the Headmaster said there would be punishment if this happened again, and left the Hall. He left one of the teachers to dismiss the assembly.

The teacher suggested that the fifth form boys might like to help the fifth form girls down from their chairs. There was a huge rush from one side of the hall to the other, with few fifth forms boys left on their own side. Not only that, but there were offers to check the laundry and sign the lists too. From what I remember fifth form boys were never short of wit. From that moment on we used to use their names for the rest of the year, or those who had been expelled, or failing that a boy's name with female sounding ending such as Simone or Adrianna, but one thing was for sure, nobody ever checked our laundry to confirm it was dirty after this episode.

The swimming pool

When I first went to Fyfield, the swimming pool was open to the air. Every springtime a group of boys volunteered to jump into it in order to extract all the leaves and accumulated rubbish and give it a good pre-season clean out. I never knew how they managed it, but it was crystal clear to swim in within about a week. It was one of those old school traditions. It was also a boy thing - girls never did it. A small crowd used to go and watch too. The Headmaster took charge, giving orders and supervising from the sidelines in a most jovial manner. It was probably the first thing that signalled that spring had arrived. The pool had a small hedge around the perimeter. It was very chilly to swim in, but that never deterred any of us from Easter onwards. The fun of being able to swim made us oblivious to the weather.

In consultation with the school, a decision was made by the Friends of Fyfield, a parents' group, to get a project team going and to raise the money which would provide the pool with a roof. My Mum and Dad, along with many others, including quite a lot of my friends' parents, achieved this by working every weekend for several months one summer. It made a very big improvement. The men set about the project whilst the women ferried tools from cars to the pool and back and prepared refreshments throughout the day. For some of us it meant that we saw a lot more of our parents than we would have otherwise done. There were quite a few parents from my year working on the project, but perhaps it was their enthusiasm, for it was our first year at the school and the fact that the person organising it was the father of one of the girls in my year too.

The new roof formed a large arc across the pool and was primarily made of plastic. It changed the whole ambience of the pool. Gone were being open to the elements, the excitement of the summer season pool cleaning and shivering as you picked up your towel from the top of the hedge and slipped on your big grey outdoor coat after a quick dry.

After it was completed we had a pool-opening ceremony, in which the school thanked the parents and the first swimmers were allowed to use the pool. It seemed different. Previously when the pool was in the open air, you would be able to feel the warm sunshine and feel dazzled by the sun dancing on the water. We used to swim whatever the weather, so if it was pouring with rain it didn't put us off. It just felt as if you were part of nature. You felt lovely and warm when you got out into the air from the pool and both your body and the pool steamed, which probably demonstrated just how cold the water was. It was quiet in the surrounding fields. I've always had an affinity with lidos since, and there were many in London.

After the pool was enclosed it echoed and seemed incredibly noisy inside. This was probably to do with the curved shape of the roof. The chlorine smell lingered for longer too. But it was a lot cleaner and we could swim all year round. Swimming became a more active pastime instead of being just for pure enjoyment. Clubs were formed and pupils started to work towards lifesaving badges. An early-morning swimming club started too, which meant swimming before breakfast. I was not good enough to join it and liked swimming as a pastime, but not being organised to swim or learning to swim better. I really wasn't that competitive either.

In the early days there wasn't anyone around telling you not to run or jump into the pool. It was just one big free for all, and you were expected to take care of yourself. When there was a teacher there, they were generally preoccupied with something else, so they were only semi-supervisory in the great outdoors. Things changed after the pool was covered.

We had a few incidents though. The pool was designed with small changing areas on the poolside, one for boys and another for girls. The teaching staff used either area when the children were not able to use the pool. One day we thought it would be a good idea to grab the clothes from the changing room, so the poor teacher who had gone for a swim had to leave the pool, much to our delight, in his skimpy Speedos, in order to find his clothes, which we left just outside the pool area. He never said anything about the incident, except that when he walked past he said 'Good evening girls' and we all giggled. He knew only too well who the culprits were, but he had managed, in a few seconds, to change his anger into ambivalence. He had that certain smile that confirmed he shared the secret.

Another incident was when someone pushed the electric pool cleaner into the pool. This stopped us being able to use the pool for quite some time, and I never knew who did it. I expect it was some sort of prank, but a silly one. I remember that the Headmaster had us standing in the hall for what seemed ages until someone owned up, but nobody did. We all loved the school caretaker, so it would not have been done to upset him and we all loved swimming too. It may well have been an accident - perhaps it just rolled into the pool by itself. We all thought the brake had probably rusted over time, as nobody really had any motive to push it in. I don't think the Headmaster had even thought of this in his rush to find and punish the culprit.

One night after lights out, occupying a dormitory within easy distance of the pool, a group of girls decided they would try skinny dipping. I wasn't one of them, being too afraid of getting caught, but off they went. Soon after I saw them leave, I saw the Headmaster heading in the same direction. At least the shadowy figure looked like him. Then I saw the pool lights go on, as they usually did some time during the evening. About twenty minutes later, back came the girls wet, so it was mission accomplished. I said they were lucky not to get caught. They said it had been a very close run thing. They had had no clothes on and had to get under the water just below where the headmaster was looking out across the pool, and he hadn't spotted them. Not only that, but they then had to hunt for their dressing gowns in the pitch dark before returning and then creep back one by one, so as to not get found out. I was quite envious when I realised they had got away with it.

The orchard was close to the pool too, and I was once caught scrumping apples, along with practically every girl in my year, apart from the few goody-goodies. Our punishment was to eat apples for every meal for a whole day. They were bitter and awful. But climbing the trees had been great fun. We had only been in the orchard for about two minutes, so I think we had been very unlucky to get caught. We did try to talk our way out of it, but to no avail. Matron wasn't having any of it – 'rescuing a cat indeed!' she said. I knew we should have got our story straight when she asked what the colour the cat was, as two replied black, one black and white, one ginger, one tabby, one tortoiseshell and I went the whole hog with a Blue Siamese! She had one of her thunderous 'don't mess with me!' looks and told us she was disgusted with our behaviour. Matron being able to keep that steely-straight face was a well-mastered art.

Next morning I met Matron and she looked at me and said 'Blue Siamese?' raising her eyebrows. I kept my head down and tried to avoid too much eye contact, and said last birthday I had been given the Observer's Book of Cats. She replied 'Very well, but never do it again as you will get tummy ache'. I said 'sorry Matron' and hurried away. When the doctor next visited, he said 'Now young lady, I hear you like cats'. We spent a long time discussing tigers, lions, cheetahs, lynx etc. He had seen some of them in the wild, so he had plenty of tales to tell, and I hadn't for once!

Some time after the pool was completed, the Friends of Fyfield organised a party to thank the parents and all those who had helped with the project, so the parents and their children turned up at a small village hall somewhere in Essex around Christmas time to enjoy themselves. Every parent took some food, every child was given a present and there were some speeches and a lot of dancing and games. It was a very good evening.

I leant that well after I had left the school a gale had demolished the roof of the pool.

Apple-pie beds, splitting and camaraderie

When you first go to boarding school there are always the school initiations. Ours were pretty simple in the 1960s and nothing that was dangerous for girls. Most things were considered pranks.

The first prank I was subjected to was an apple-pie bed. It is called that because the top sheet is folded very neatly to resemble a perfectly-made bed, but when you get into it of course your legs can only go halfway down the bed. This was on my first night at school, and the girls said they wanted to find out whether I would tell, cry or laugh. They soon found out that I did fit in, as I said nothing when the teacher came in, but after she went I asked who had done it and then tipped her mattress onto the floor with her still in bed!

A further prank I was subjected to was when one of my friends confiscated a skirt from a younger pupil, cut out her name tape and took a name tape out of my jumper, which I never wore, and sewed it into the smaller girl's skirt. I was puzzled for about half an hour as to why it didn't fit and was on the verge of accusing the school laundry service of shrinking my skirt when I found out what had happened. We fell about laughing. It was some time after the Head of Girls had done her skirt inspection, and I must have kept on about the unfairness of it all. Apparently it was done to shut me up!

Another prank was played on one of the teachers by the boys in the class, and I had nothing to do with it. It was the upper set for Maths. There were only two girls, one named Susan, me and twelve boys. The usual routine was that the Maths teacher came in, dumped his very large briefcase on the table, turned round and walked to the back of the room to shut the door. It was a very warm summer's day and the windows were open. As his back was turned one of the lads tied a piece of string to the case and lowered it out of the window. He went to the desk and was puzzled to see his case had gone. He then went to the open window and said 'very funny' and went out to collect it, by which time of course it had been hoisted back into place and rested on the desk. Later, when he turned his back the second time, the same thing happened, but this time someone on the lower floor had taken it into a room before it got to the ground. This time the teacher was really annoyed. He gave us a lecture saying it was just too hot to be chasing up and down, the first time had been funny but the joke was wearing thin.

The result was that the whole class lost a house point and had to do one hundred quadratic equations before the end of the day and hand it in, otherwise we would lose another house point. We all got together in the break and shared them out to do six or so each and the culprit the residue, with the best students re-checking our work in case we had gone wrong. They were handed in at lunchtime and the teacher said he was impressed with all fourteen of us getting every one right.

There was one very attractive young female teacher in our school. She had model-like features and a warm personality, and all the boys liked her. One day two young lads ran away from school, and as usual the teachers went out to find them. Nobody really got very far because it was a very long way to run to anywhere, but of course some people hadn't worked this out! This rather lovely teacher found the two boys hiding in a ditch, gave them a motherly cuddle and brought them back to school. Of course the much older boys were a bit jealous, and the next day it was announced that ten older boys from the school had run away. They ended up losing a house point instead of a motherly cuddle because, as the Headmaster said, they were the ones who should be setting a good example to follow. I remember the School Council discussing it and finding it quite amusing. I think things changed after I left, because I have heard tales of pupils reaching London and all sorts of places after their running-away antics.

Do you remember in primary school there was a nasty rhyme? It went: 'Tell-tale tit, your tongue will split and all the little puppy dogs will have a bit'. So when you went to boarding school the term *split on someone* means to betray, tell on, shop, sing, grass, give away, peach or squeal. Splitting or telling tales was considered totally unforgivable. Once you had committed this breach of trust, you had the label of goody-goody and had to do something pretty spectacular to gain acceptance again by your peers. The opposite happened when you gained a reputation for not splitting, you could immediately be trusted - simple.

There were a few splitters in our year, though I can't ever remember doing the dirty on anyone. It was the silent school code. I do remember the whole class being punished for the one person who didn't own up at times, but we didn't drop them in it even if we knew. There was a lot of pressure on them to do the right thing and own up. I even got a few punishments because I never split, but in my eyes it was better to get punished than end up being a labelled a goody-goody.

With regard to the field walking episode, where we had to walk the perimeter of the field for talking after lights out at 11.30 pm, a classmate split on me for giggling and acting the fool and it was one of the reasons I had to do it for four nights. Another classmate who also had to do it with me kept on about what her parents would say if they ever found out. This was good information, and I used it to my advantage. I often used to say to her 'can I borrow...' and if she said no, which invariably she did, I'd say 'Oh it will be such a shame when your parents find out about the field walking!' She always gave in, and I always thought that if the boot was on the other foot I'd say 'go ahead tell then' and take my chances. So you see I wasn't really in the good category at all, more manipulative I suppose. Quite frankly it had never bothered me what my parents would think, and I doubted very much whether they would really be concerned about me talking.

Eventually, I told my parents what had happened anyway, and my Dad said 'There is nothing wrong with talking, as long as it is about something interesting. The only problem you had was getting caught'. I could always rely on Dad for good analysis of a problem and later I hoped that I could be like my parents; nothing really bothered them too much. They always said it was the really big things in life you should concern yourself with.

By the time we had got to the last year of school, we had learnt to get on with one another, in the main. The prefects were an especially nice, thoughtful group of mature and responsible people. There were not that many of us left in our year group, as some had left the year beforehand and a few in Year 2.

This self-imposed or handed-down idea of sorting things out for yourself and not telling tales all the time really worked. We did however have the common sense to know that if someone was doing something really foolish we must get help.

The library, books and magazines

When I first went to Fyfield, the main teaching block and school hall had not long been built and the library was in a small room to the side of the glass doors corridor. Later it moved to what was for years the common room, but by this time it had expanded and was a fair size for a school library. The old music room became a common room and the music room was relocated to one end of the quadrangle.

The old library became the humanities room. This was a new subject that we had been fortunate enough to miss out on. I just thought that if you were going to study something it warranted your full attention and you needed to cover the subject in depth. I would have hated having my favourite Geography watered down. It comprised Citizenship, Geography, History, RE and Sociology, giving students the opportunity to develop a greater understanding of the world around them.

The non-fiction area of the library was fairly substantial and the fiction area a lot smaller. There were books on practically everything you wanted and a comprehensive reference section too. The non-fiction section was catalogued according to the Dewey Decimal Classification System, a proprietary system of library classification developed by Melvil Dewey in 1876. The system attempts to organize all knowledge into ten main classes. These are each further subdivided into ten divisions and each division into ten sections, giving ten main classes, 100 divisions and 1000 sections. It sounds complicated, but I understood it as I was the Head Librarian in the last year of school and used to do most of the filing myself. I had an excellent memory and still do, but filing most things myself and knowing who had what books out enabled me to locate things pretty quickly.

One of the advantages of being Head Librarian was that

I got to choose most of the new books that came from Essex County Library on the book swap, and some of the new library editions too. If I had a favourite fiction author, I used to order the whole series of books, just to keep my own reading supply going. I was also allowed to make recommendations about which magazines we should have, as we had a large selection of mainly monthly magazines. In 1969 my favourite was the National Geographic, which I liked for the spectacular photography. I have always liked travel and social history too, so this periodical filled my mind with far-off lands and exotic animals. I made up my mind that I was going to travel as soon as I could. Even now I read a lot of books and magazines about the places I visit before travelling.

More boys looked at magazines than girls, so I chose magazines on cars, aeroplanes, agriculture, yachting etc. I liked cars too, and had made up my mind to learn to drive as soon as it was possible.

I do remember at Fyfield that the most looked-at magazine by the Fifth Form boys was 'Practical Photography', and it was often the magazine with pages torn out. I can't ever remember that many boys being interested in photography though, or in fact taking many photographs.

We had newspapers every day, but in those days they were only broadsheets. Nobody had yet printed the smaller size paper or anything in colour, as they do today. They were huge papers that you couldn't really hold to read, you had to lay them flat on a table and stand up to read them.

Everything was black and white. The ink from the newspapers made your hands so black that they had to be washed after reading them. It also came off the paper and went all over your clothes, unless you read at a distance. That's why when a paper was put out across a table it was left for the next person to come and read it. I remember questioning at the time why adults would buy a newspaper as they seemed quite boring, although the landing on the moon and fashion captured my imagination. Papers nowadays are very different from the way they were in the 1960s. One thing I do vividly remember was that most of the content of a newspaper was actually news. There was very little about celebrities. There was the odd scandal, but in the main there was far more politics and far more sport, and all the papers had exactly the same format. 'The Times' used to be left open on the table and one by one each reader would fill in a word of the crossword, so by the end of the day it was either complete or near to it. I also liked supplements which had good photographs. The library was a place to escape to at Fyfield when you needed a bit of peace and quiet. Fortunately too it was adjacent to Queens's dormitory, so it was only a very short stroll for me.

Sometimes I was curious as to why a book had been borrowed from the library, so I used to have a good look at it myself. Boys used to borrow mainly non-fiction books and girls fiction, although the vast majority of regular library users were boys.

We never had any childish or children's books at Fyfield. They were all young adult or adult books and the fiction authors were Nevil Shute, Graham Greene and Ernest Hemingway, for example. There were plenty of coursework books for English students too; my favourite was Dylan Thomas' *Under Milk Wood*, with Mrs Organ Morgan forever in my mind.

I read a lot at Fyfield, and that skill never left me. Reading is still one of my pastimes and I manage to read around thirty or more books a year, although of course over the years my reading has developed and I have discovered many good authors, some of them modern and some American. I own some very lovely first editions and have some interesting books in my possession, such as very early editions of 'House at Pooh Corner', 'Cranford', 'East Lynne', Edward Lear's rhymes and early Enid Blyton books, all of which have been presents to me over the years. I also still have a book given to me by my Dad when I was eight, 'The Secret Garden' by Frances Hodgson Burnett. I have read it many times. I am not that keen on paperback books, but I love a hardback. Electronic books are handy for holidays but do not have the same feel or meaning to me as a proper book.

Most of my reading is also about travel, although I have always been keen on biographies too. However my favourite places are those very musty old bookshops. I've found a lovely one in Wimbledon, one in the Cotswolds and another in York. They are the type of place where the people running them know every corner of their own store and they are readers too. Often I've purchased a book and the owner says, 'Good choice, I've read it'. They are so much nicer than modern shops and you get bargains. The only disadvantage is that books in those days did not have or had lost their magnificent dust jackets and there is skill in producing some of those you see today. I can be fascinated by the way a dust-jacket tries to tell its own story before you start to read it, and I think it is a very important part of the book.

During my working life I read a lot of books, at work mainly about drugs and precursor chemicals, because that was the subject I was working on. They probably are the most irritatingly inaccurate books I have ever read, primarily because the author was either pro or anti illegal drugs, so the books were primarily based on opinion and not fact. The only ones that could be regarded as interesting were those that concentrated on the chemical or medicinal side, as they were factual books. I could read a fairly lengthy book in an evening but developed a habit of using a highlighter pen to remember a few significant items, especially those I considered useful in meetings. Thank goodness highlighters were not around in the 1960s.

I am also a true magazine junky, but the topics over years change and I am now into walking, photography, DIY and travel.

Saturday evening films

Before I went to Fyfield I used to go to the Saturday morning pictures at the Granada in Walthamstow, which was a very good morning's entertainment for 6d. It was one of the highlights of my young life.

My love of film goes back a very long way. My Nan

worked in Wardour Street for Pathé, and later MGM followed by Arthur J Rank. It was a centre of the British film industry with the big production and distribution companies having their headquarters there. In the early days my Nan was a cutter and sticker, joining the very early films together; later she progressed to subtitles, changing foreign language films into English. She worked on a lot of the newsreels during the Second World War. Her mother was Italian and my Granddad's mother was of Prussian decent, so Nan's language skills provided a good income. She was a very hard and disciplined worker too.

Every Saturday evening at Fyfield we had a full-length film to watch. In the early days we had a short film followed by a feature film, but towards the end of the 1960s we, like many cinemas, dispensed with the short films and just went for feature films.

For some reason, missing the film was considered a very big punishment. Detention was run for the same time as the film, in a room adjacent to the School Hall. Fifth formers had the option to attend; it was compulsory for all lower years.

I suppose television wasn't all that popular as most of the programmes shown were at one end of the spectrum, for young children, or the other end, programmes for adults. Very few programmes appealed to teenagers and I can only think of a couple, 'Top of the Pops' being the most popular, closely followed by 'Dr Who'. This probably accounts for why the Saturday film was an 'event'.

In the last year I was at Fyfield, 1969-1970, there were eighteen film evenings.

The films were rated in a school poll and came in this order, starting with the most popular:

The Diary of Anne Frank (70% rating it as 'excellent')
Carry On Doctor
Colditz
A Matter of Life and Death
Prince Valiant
The Wreck of the Mary Deare
Rhino
Ringo's Golden Pistol
Invasion Quartet
It Takes a Thief
War Waggon
Call Me Bwana
The Third Man
Ringer
Kill or Cure
Kind Hearts and Coronets
Sheepman
L'il Abner (12% rating as 'excellent' and 68% 'poor'.

Each film evening a log recorded the number of people who were absent. There were only five pupils absent from the showing of Anne Frank (1959), which is not that surprising as the book 'The Diary of Anne Frank' (1968) was on our GCE English reading list. It was compulsory to study English. I am sure the film added something to our understanding of the harrowing story about Anne, a young

Jewish girl who, with her family and their friends, was forced into hiding in an attic in Nazi-occupied Amsterdam.

The film second on the list of popularity was 'Carry on Doctor', which was probably popular on three accounts: the first that it was full of sexual innuendo, the second that it featured a scantily-clad and saucy character (Nurse Sandra May) and the third that everyone loves a film which has revenge as part of the plot. The film closes with the patients' revenge on Dr Tinkle and the formidable matron because of their conspiracy against a Dr Kilmore. I suppose that having a doctor called Kilmore seemed funny to us at that age. Having a doctor called Tinkle was even funnier, as well as having a formidable matron, or in fact any sort of matron we could identify with.

Forty-one people chose not to see 'Invasion Quartet'. The plot was about four undercover agents who travelled by train behind Nazi lines in a plan to disarm a huge German gun aimed at the port of Dover. The creators of Invasion Quartet piled joke upon joke by having the Nazis portrayed as bumbling buffoons. Having previously seen the film Anne Frank, this obviously did not appeal to our sense of humour.

The least popular film was L'il Abner, probably because it was a 1959 musical and I think musicals were the least liked of all films when we were at school. I remember that some years prior to this, one of the films shown was 'The Sound of Music', and very few liked it. I remember along with everyone else being bored before the first sight of a mountain.

If a film had a complicated plot or a vast cast, it was

often too difficult to engage and keep the attention of schoolchildren, so what might appeal to the younger children often didn't appeal to the older ones and vice versa. It must have been difficult to try and find medium ground for 11-16 year olds. It was also difficult to please both sexes. I remember the excitement of the boys when 'Colditz' was shown. I also remember that the girls preferred the romance in 'A Matter of Life and Death'.

A new English teacher joined Fyfield midway through my time there and introduced many of us to what is now called 'Media Studies', although back in the sixties it was referred to as Additional English Studies. It was probable from the outset that as watching film was part of the study, the topic would prove popular. The subject was intended to develop topics to expand research, problem-solving and creative skills. It also widened debating skills through addressing contemporary issues.

All the years sat in rows and as you went into the hall girls sat on the left and boys on the right according to the year they were in, so by the Fifth Form you had progressed to the very back row and Year Five could also mix, so mostly there were couples. Many years after leaving school I was reading an old pupil website with accounts from pupils that left the school in the eighties, a long time after I was a pupil there, and they were still reminiscing about being barred from watching the film if they misbehaved, so the tradition went on for many years, like many other Fyfield traditions.

Rather strangely too, the word 'film' was pronounced differently in the 1960s at school. It was 'filim' in sound and very different to the sound nowadays in England, although still a Scottish way.

My favourite lessons

I have written in part about my least favourite lessons, needlework and domestic science, but not yet about those I loved.

One of my favourite subjects was Mathematics. This was really because of damage limitation - not much could get me into trouble. There were no sharp objects involved (except for the compass incident), no pancakes or electrical equipment involved, just good old H E Parrs mathematics books, numbers one to five , part I and II for each year of school, an exercise book and some graph paper. Best of all was the smashing enthusiastic teacher, who knew everything about mathematics.

Although I never did that well academically at school, I did achieve a very reasonable grade in Mathematics and ten years after leaving I acquired a good grade at both Mathematics and Modern Mathematics in GCE. Most of this was down to the teacher at Fyfield. I was quite shy about asking anything in class, especially as there was only one other girl in the class and all the rest were boys. The boys seemed to know everything when it came to maths, or perhaps I was just slow to understand. However the teacher always used to say 'Don't just sit there wondering – ask!' He had such a lot of patience. I immediately understood and took to formal geometry and any type of equation, but when it came to looking up the tables for logarithms and anti-logarithms, I often got muddled up, which led to a lot of nonsensical answers and hysterical laughter from the boys.

These are questions that were in my book (for a 13-year-old):

When petrol cost 4s 6d a gallon and oil is 6s a quart, a motorcyclist finds that the cost of petrol and oil for 10000 miles is £6. When the price of petrol goes up to 5s and that of oil to 6s 6d, the cost for 1000 miles is £6 12s and 6d. Find out how many gallons of petrol and quarts of oil he uses for the 1000 miles.

My answer was nothing; he walks, because if it's all going up by that much he probably can't afford it. The teacher's response was '"what do I pay you for?' which confused me even more! It was just one of his little sayings. But that was a product of my young, logical mind and coming from a very poor part of London.

Then there was the compass incident. Desks were small and equipment took up quite a bit of it. First the ruler fell to the floor and the maths teacher said 'what was that? Pick it up, silly girl.' Then the book went over the edge, again he said ' Oh Diane for goodness sake pick it up', then the compass went over the edge with the point down and it went straight into my foot. With his back to us, he said 'I don't want to know. Whatever it is it can stay there'. Half an hour later he came walking towards me and said 'Diane what's wrong with your foot?' Although I had kicked the compass out the way, my foot was bleeding and I sat there with one red sock and one white one. He said 'Why didn't you say something?' I replied 'Well, you said you didn't want to know'. Looking at the person next to me, he said 'Susan, take her to Sick Bay, I am beginning to think that you are all completely stupid'.

He had a point, because the following day I got into trouble for using the protractor back to front and came up with a whole page of wrong answers. I remember him saying 'You must have known, after all your answers are all less than 90 degrees and we were measuring those that are bigger, wake up, the clue is in the title of this lesson, 'Obtuse Angles', so what would be studying if they were less Diane?'

I answered 'Mmm... acute, sir'.

'Hooray she knows something, result!'

To be fair it could have happened to anyone, although I had been struggling to read the numbers backwards all morning and still the penny hadn't dropped.

I had a natural affinity with Geography, which really means if you like something enough you will remember it and learn more too. I can't remember any part of physical Geography that I disliked. Perhaps it was because I enjoyed being outdoors so much. Everything about the land, countries, population, what the countries produced, was fascinating. I looked forward to this subject more than any other and wished I had more than two periods a week to study it. I always used to ask for the back issues of National Geographic when they were being thrown away and supplement my knowledge with their articles. In the last year this double period of Geography was on a Wednesday, which gave me something to look forward to, and my easy day just happened to be a Friday, with a double private study period at the end of a day. This meant that prep could be done really early, and that gave me the whole weekend to enjoy.

Rural Science was a wonderful subject, because I found both the practical and theory easy to understand. It had a sense of logic to it. Once you had mastered crop rotation, photosynthesis and what different compounds did to the plants, basically you were there. Not only that but you could nibble all afternoon at what you had grown. We were divided into two groups and Polly took my group. There was nothing nicer on a warm summer's day than standing there in your PE kit, with the boys in theirs, trying to listen to what Polly had to say about the art of 'gardening' with a fag sticking out the side of her mouth, so you understood about one word in three. She was less interested in the subject than we were and disappeared into the shed to light yet another fag about every five minutes, whilst we had sword fights with the Dutch hoes and the boys used the watering hose to invent the 'Miss Wet T-shirt' competition. Oh the days of when shorts were just that short and very tight! It was really a wonder that we could ever garden in them, as we couldn't even comfortably bend over in them! Polly never took the subject very seriously and neither did we, it was just a fun afternoon for all.

I'm sorry to the girl, you know who you are, for putting a stick right through your lovely neat row of lettuces so they came up straggly and all over the place after you went to so much trouble to get them straight with the chalk line for the second year running, but it was a dare.

Human Biology was fun, as I was the only pupil to take the subject. Some others took Biology, but not Human Biology. I sat in the front on my own whilst the teacher pottered around doing various jobs and a bit of marking whilst also trying to drum some knowledge into my head. It was quite nice having the attention. He always started off by saying, "Well, what shall we learn today?" and my response was always the same – "What can I dissect and label?" Now there were two things wrong with this strategy, one being that he never paid any attention to the National Curriculum and the second was that we were soon running out of things to dissect. This probably accounts for why at the first attempt at O level, my results were poor. However I did achieve a reasonably good grade on the second attempt, primarily because my fixation with dissection had lapsed and I had stumbled across Gray's Anatomy. Well, that and not playing around with the skeleton, as one did.

Biology was the same, as I had been fairly reasonable at the human side of things but hadn't paid enough attention to other areas. Again, a re-sit enabled me to get another good grade at O level.

During the last two years of school a new subject was introduced, at that time called Additional English Studies. It was mainly about the study of propaganda, advertising and films. This enabled us to watch a lot of films that were not mainstream. It was probably the start of my personal grasp on analysis, a skill I developed throughout my career. I can remember watching a film called 'Wild Strawberries' which made you think about the difficulties in life and self-discovery. The main character gradually begins to accept his past, present and impending death. Until that time I had always seen film just for pure enjoyment, much the same as watching television. I had never analysed or really thought about anything I had watched before. This was probably the start of my love of film outside the popular range. By the time I left, I also had a fair grasp of advertising. I learnt that advertising is a form of communication that persuades people to do something by way of delivering a message, like buy their products or continue to use their product due to its merits, with the result of making money. It involves the repetition of an image or product name in an effort to associate certain qualities with the brand in the minds of people.

We studied an advert for a well-known tomato soup to try and understand that commercial advertisers often seek to generate increased consumption of their product through branding and by using television adverts that deliver subliminal messages, as it was thought that subliminal stimuli activate specific regions of the brain despite participants being unaware. We were then asked to write down some adjectives after watching the soup advert and asked how we felt. I think we said warm, cosy, family etc. We were shown the advert broken down by very slow frames, and in between the bowls of soup you saw a shot of a warm and happy family, with children sitting at a table in front of an open fire eating their soup served by mother. There was a further advert for a well-known fizzy drink that we studied too. This subject opened up a whole new world for me, and taught me to think beyond what I was told was fact. Up to this point I had more or less believed everything adults told me, but this made me think. Advertisers in the UK are no longer allowed to use this subliminal advertising.

We had a theme of war and among the films I watched were 'Once There Was a War', a Danish film about life in Copenhagen during the closing stages of World War Two, 'Culloden', which portrayed the 1746 Battle of Culloden which resulted in the British Army's destruction of the Jacobite uprising and, in the words of the narrator, 'tore apart forever the clan system of the Scottish Highlands'. There was also 'A Time Out of War', about Civil War soldiers on two sides of a river who decide to call a cease-fire for a few hours. Other titles were Hell is for Heroes, Merrill's Marauders, The War Game, The Long, the Short and the Tall, The Wild Ones, The Leather Boys, Incident at Owl Creek, Shane and Lord of the Flies. This film was good for both English and also additional English, as it was on our compulsory reading list.

The only exam I had a bad grade in (I never bothered with it again) was Medieval History. I was just so upset at getting a poor grade of 8, but was not ungraded. Today is it equivalent to a GCSE at grade B. Again we had to answer questions and found that we hadn't been taught the full curriculum, so I attempted to answer two questions I hadn't even studied. In the end the teacher looked into it and found he had been given the wrong papers to teach from. I gave up. I am sure the world hasn't suffered because I failed to gain a good grade O level in Medieval History. I did though later take an O level in Social History. I would also say though that I like historical dramas and I am still an avid reader of the Medieval period, and I especially enjoy photographing Medieval architecture.

Signing out, and places around Fyfield

I had been used to finding my own way around London without the hindrance of a companion, without having permission, without having to say where I was going or how long I was going to be, and only having a rough idea of when I was going to return. I never had to say who I was going to be with or who or what I was going to visit either, so imagine my dismay when I arrived at my first opportunity to leave the school premises and found that there were rules.

When I first went to Fyfield, signing out was a big adventure, but I was disappointed to find that you had to sign out with someone and were not allowed to go out on your own. I thought this was going to impede my explorations. By the time I went to Fyfield most of the girls already had their signing-out buddies, so I had to wait until someone had an argument and a temporary falling-out before I was asked. Just my luck too that she was a rule maker and safety advisor to boot, who had been well advised on all the things that could happen to us.

So with sturdy shoes, well wrapped up in my school raincoat, money counted twice in my little purse hidden in a secret pocket, a torch (yes a torch in the middle of the day!) and a stern reminder that we were not to talk to strangers, we set off on my very first expedition, which was to the village shop to get some sweets. It doesn't sound that exciting, but it was, because instead of going along the road we went via the footpath. Not only that, but I felt in some way now accepted. From then on I went out with others all the time and was never left out. I had guaranteed this by sharing my sweets on the way back to school.

On our way back through fields and hedgerows we often stopped to pick wild flowers, which were in abundance. We used to give them to our favourite teachers. I remember once that one of the teachers said they were very nice, but I had picked deadly nightshade, so to be sure to go and wash my hands, and she was sorry but they had to go outside as they were quite pungent. She made quite sure that she hadn't hurt my feelings as I had tried hard to do something nice.

We created our own landmarks around Fyfield so that when we talked about places we all knew where we meant.

Places of note in the village were:

The Gypsy Mead tea room was a long building which looked posh. Anywhere where you could go to tea was posh. For years we walked past it. It always seemed empty. Then one day one of our friends said she was going to the tea room with her parents, and if I liked I too could come along if I asked school for permission. I duly got permission and went down to the village with my friend and her parents. It was her birthday celebration. It was posh and empty and quite disappointing, but it had satisfied my curiosity. I never wanted to sit at a round table right in the middle of that empty and echoing tea room. That wasn't a birthday treat in my mind, it was an ordeal. I never wanted to go there again.

The village shop was small, but very modern in 1965. It was packed with all sorts of supplies. It was the sort of place that local residents avoided when Fyfield pupils were around because they got crushed in the scramble and it was noisy, or I should say we were noisy. No matter what the shopkeeper said we ignored it or were oblivious to his requests, such as being quiet, queuing nicely, not all going into the shop at once and not using it to shelter from the rain when we were not buying anything. Oh how we laughed at him. He always threatened to tell the Headmaster and rarely did, except on one occasion. We nicknamed him 'Moany moany'. After his visit to our Headmaster yet another layer of guidance was added to that very extensive list, which resembled the Encyclopaedia Britannica. One rule was that a prefect was to supervise children in and out of the shop!

The river flowed under the bridge in the centre of the village, along Queen Street, past the Queen's Head public house. We often used to go and look at the ducks on the pond. It was a very picturesque place and lovely on a summer's day. Occasionally during our later years we went to do a bit of teacher-spotting. You had to guess what teacher would be in the pub, who they were with, and what they were drinking to score a point which was added up to three points a visit through the term, but you lost all your points if you ever saw a policeman riding a bike. Those were the rules!

St Nicholas' Church was the local Church of England church we attended, sometimes twice on a Sunday because you were allowed to get up very early to go to the 7.30 service before breakfast. We did this on lovely summer mornings and got back in time for breakfast. You approached it across a large common. It was a fairly small and pretty church and pupils from Fyfield generally made up most of the congregation. We walked from school, taking the public footpath across to Willingale Road.

One of the places we often visited was the old airfield. If you came out of school and turned towards Ongar, crossed the road and turned right, then immediately opposite was a footpath that wound its way round to a disused airfield. The runways were still there during the 1960s, made up of a concrete patch landing strip and plenty of grass around the perimeter. We used to run up and down the runways making aeroplane noises and generally acted stupid, but it was fun, in the middle of nowhere and quiet. For some reason a lot of our year used to go there. It was here that we played war games with imaginary conversations with the pilots. Some took the roles of planes themselves, demonstrating a wide range of aircraft noises, while others were gunners. There were never too many of us to join in. The local farmer used to come by with his dog and we always asked him if it was OK to play and he always used to say 'Why not?' and stand and watch us.

Another farmer came past who had been out shooting rabbits, but he only used to say hello. We were never told that we shouldn't be there or had to go. It felt as if it was ours. Once to our amazement we saw a very small plane arrive, and when it had shut down its engine we went over to have a look at it.

If you ventured into Ongar and took the footpath across from the bus stop outside where the toilets were located you could get down to the river. On lovely summer afternoons we sat by the river, and sometimes we paddled about in it too. It was just lovely to lie on your back, occasionally talk and listen to the running water. The hours in the summer sun seemed endless. We never saw anyone there; it was ours. Mind you, reality quickly brought us down to earth after a ride back in the school van.

Spains Wood was another of our playgrounds. You went by bicycle to Fyfield, turned right and went a couple of miles until you got to the woods. Many couples went there, but there were also a whole group of fifth formers who used to go there just to sit around and talk.

The seasons and school terms

The school year started with the new intake of pupils and returners starting the new school year in the first week of September. It was a long term which ended around the 19th of December. New pupils had to quickly get to grips with the different routine of a boarding school, as the nights were dark by five o'clock. It was often cold and frosty by the time we went to supper and very cold and damp by the time prep had finished. Despite the dark and damp, nobody wore a coat and very few a jumper.

During the winter months we often played hockey, and by the time we went in to shower our bodies had turned bright red with the cold and wet. We had to Vaseline our lips, otherwise they cracked in the cold. I remember quite vividly crows making that early-morning noise that lets you know they are about, a very winter noise.

The autumn term saw the Halloween Dance and in October Speech Day, which was a day when most of the school leavers of the previous year returned, and the carol service, swiftly followed by Christmas parties and Christmas lunch. I remember walking to the dormitory from the school block and seeing our hot breath steaming as we chatted to one another. We didn't really seem to notice the cold at that age. With weekends home, the time between September and Christmas seemed to fly past.

We returned for the spring term in early January and stayed on the winter timetable until half term, when we then adjusted to the summer timetable. This term seemed to drag on, especially if Easter fell in April and not March. We had a music competition on St Cecelia's day. Most of the school's overseas trips took place during the Easter holidays.

It must have rained at some time during the five years I was at school, but I really never remember getting soaking wet. I put that down to finding a sheltered route between buildings or staying put until it has stopped. Perhaps life was just too good to notice rain.

The summer term was lovely by contrast, with the steady sound of the mower and the perpetual smell of new-mown grass. I can hear in my head to this day the rhythm of that mower and the way the sound changed as it turned at the corners of the very large field.

Lessons were over in the afternoon, and there was still time to sign out after tea or to go and play rounders on the field after prep. If it was a hot and cloudless day, prep was cancelled and it was just one long session of swimming and athletics on the field as we prepared ourselves for the house competitions and Sports Day. We played rounders and softball and often watched the boys in a cricket match. I often scored for these matches. There were very many long cricket matches, as it was as popular with staff as it was with pupils. We all practised athletics incessantly to improve our own personal best or just to have a go at trying out an athletics activity and to compete for our house during sports day. I tried most things and only excelled at the high jump. I could also throw the discus and shot putt, but I really wanted to be able to throw the javelin. Running never really interested me as I got older because at fifteen I was becoming very self-conscious about my large breasts and somehow it never seemed to be very ladylike to run and get hot and sweaty. Not only that, but since my early days nobody had ever really chased after me or been horrible to me. I had lost the will to escape.

I couldn't wait to get up in the mornings on summer days, and at weekends it seemed as if time stood still so that you could enjoy it. When we were young we sat on the field and made very long daisy chains. Then when we were a bit older we packed in activities and during the last year we would talk, read books and go on bike rides. When I say bike rides, the bikes belonged to the boys and we just sat on the handlebars for excursions out into the wider countryside.

Saturday 30th May 1970 was the date of a Swimming Gala held at Harlow Pool. The swimming gala was quite a grand affair with all of us being taken to the pool with parents as spectators. I never competed much, and only during my early years. I did love swimming very much, but not racing and I definitely did not like being seen in a fairly juvenile swimming costume after the age of thirteen. I was only a spectator in the last few years. However it was a tradition that the leaving year would perform an entertainment for the rest of the school and parents after the gala had officially ended. I remember ours was called 'It's a Frank Production' - someone banged a gong at the end of the pool, in a take-off of the Rank Organisation film titles.

As I remember, our school, although very small, had a very good reputation for sports in general, but particularly for swimming, taking part in the West Essex Championships and putting swimmers forward to represent the Essex Schools team.

Quite a few of us took part in a sponsored swim for charity. I was sponsored mostly by my family and one or two friends at school, but I didn't know anyone at home, so my list was probably one of the shortest. I managed to finish the swim. I think I raised the lowest amount of money and felt quite bad about it. I was quite upset that I didn't know anyone to add to my list and it made me quite miserable when I heard of the amounts that others had been sponsored for.

Jack, the school caretaker, saw me looking sorrowful and asked me what was wrong, and I told him. He said "Never mind the amount, it's doing something for others that's important" and added his name to my list. Then he got a lot of the other domestic staff to do likewise. The amount of money was still very small, but at least the number of names on the list was significant and it made me feel a whole lot better. So you can see that Fyfield was like one big family that took care of one another.

I wasn't a competitive swimmer but more a daydreamy distance swimmer, without any style whatsoever. I went to swimming club once, and the teacher told me I had many things wrong with my style, but I really couldn't be bothered with it and quickly realised that aiming for perfection was seriously going to ruin my enjoyment of it, so it was my first and last time. We spent a lot of time diving to pick up a rubber brick from the bottom of the pool and towing someone in pyjamas around, all in the name of lifesaving. I couldn't really see why anyone would need to pick up a brick from the bottom of the pool, and why on earth would anyone be wearing pyjamas near water? Not only that, but the teacher bellowed her instructions. I swear that I have never since ever met anyone who could shout that loud.

The pool was pandemonium, with fifteen pupils. I was so overwhelmed by the noise that I decided I had better things to do with my time and there were going to be more than enough lifesavers, as ours was only the first class and there were six more to follow. My days of scary chlorine red eyes had ended. I never took part in any competitions and only in the sketch when I was in the last year of school, and that was only because I didn't want to be the only one who wasn't in it.

This was followed in June by the Friends of Fyfield hosting the School Fete, and there was an Open Day for all during July. Sometimes old pupils returned and it was good to see them and hear about what they had been doing.

The fete on 21st June 1970 was a day never to be forgotten. It was a lovely summer's day and the fete got off to a jolly good start, but it soon deteriorated into quite a farce. Firstly my Dad ran a hoopla stall. What could possibly go wrong with that? Well, having beer as a prize was one thing, followed by the hoops not quite fitting over the rings he had carefully crafted. Someone complained about both the rings and the alcohol. So my Dad spent some considerable time, after borrowing a file from Jack the caretaker, making the blocks of wood smaller, whilst my Mum wrote 'Lemonade' on labels to stick over the beer bottles. My Dad quickly became very popular with the boys and surprisingly enough money was raised and the stock ran out, rapidly. So rapidly that after thirty minutes the stall had closed.

The second catastrophe was down to the Friends of Fyfield. They had spent some considerable time on an irrigation project to water the tennis courts and cricket pitches. This had involved laying underground pipes across the field, together with all associated junctions, valves, drains and spraying points. We should have known that disaster was about to strike when they announced some weeks earlier that a demonstration of their completed work would be given on Fete Day. Well the good outcome of the project was that the system did in fact work and worked well. It gave the ground a thorough soaking in a matter of minutes, even seconds. At the end of the fete day traditionally parents brought a picnic where both pupils and parents sat by their cars with blankets spread, laden with scrumptious goodies. They did so on this day, but not for long because the irrigation demonstration had just started when various mothers got to their feet screaming that their frocks were wet through. Food was quickly piled onto car bonnets and children sought refuge in cars. The situation wasn't really helped that much by my Dad standing in a puddle spouting on about pounds per square inch and generally giving a lecture on water pressure and where they had gone wrong. That was really the trouble; my Dad, a laboratory technician, was a scientific clever clogs who was more interested in the problem than keeping his feet dry.

Did we laugh? Yes! Especially as he had been one of the party that had installed it! It was another one of those days when my Mum said 'Oh Ronnie, you could have said before turning the thing on'. He replied 'You'd have thought it was sports day and not fete day, the way everybody sprinted off and jumped into their cars'. He was fairly amused by the whole farce. Most people were not.

Inter-House competitions and club events

Each of the four houses, Abbess, Aythorpe, Beauchamp and

Berners, had about 60 pupils. For some unknown reason, pupils of similar abilities, like those who were good at music or sport, seemed to be in one house, although it generally followed that family members were in the same house.

For the most part I can only remember the activities that I took part in during 1969-1970 and their outcomes.

The inter-house competitions were just that - competitive. Very competitive. I was in Beauchamp House and our most outstanding success was in the House points shield, which we won every week except one during my last year of 69/70. It was almost becoming a tradition to collect the shield, tie our green ribbon on it and hang it back on the wall. As a prefect I collected it every third week or so.

We also surprised other Houses by winning the Cross Country Cup in 1969, scoring just one point more than the favourite House to win, Berners. I remember this because I was marshalling at the event. Perhaps I accidentally sent someone the wrong way?

The netball competition was tied with Aythorpe House after a very wet and cold season of sport. I was the Assistant Goal Shooter, but unfortunately most of the goal defenders in the other houses were tall, which was a disadvantage to us unless I got the ball quickly and had a clear chance at the net. I could move about quite smartly and my friend Christine was the House Captain, so I always got a place in the team during the last year and it was always in my favourite position. That was a clear advantage of being in the fifth year - that you took part in most teams if you wanted to, or conversely you opted out of sport altogether.

We came second in the Hockey Cup, also 1969, although it was difficult for us having so many girls in the school team who often went to play away, leaving us short of players for the inter-house matches. Aythorpe just managed to secure the Hockey Cup. I too played for the school as a hockey reserve in the last year, but only when someone was injured, which was quite often. Some of the injuries were quite serious, like losing teeth or getting a bleeding nose or head. I was glad I played on the wing and out of harm's way, especially in games of mixed hockey as the boys could be vicious, but the girls more so. That year we lost every under 16-game, but mostly the games were cancelled due to adverse weather, so perhaps our poor results could have been due to a lack of practice. Or it might just have been my presence.

Beauchamp didn't win the Drama Festival, which went to Abbess House. We were doing very well when one of our leading players was taken ill and we could not replace them at such short notice. Then we lost out in the football to Berners too. In fact we came second in quite a lot of the activities, but never last.

Two years prior to 1969, drama was not very popular. Two very successful musicals were produced, but pupils lacked acting skill and there was a general feeling of apathy towards drama despite the enthusiasm of a talented few. Then two drama clubs were started, improvisation for the juniors and a club for the older pupils. The middle school put on three good one-act plays. The final event of the year was a production of a three-act comedy called 'Caught

Napping' by the Fifth Form. It was the first time a form had attempted a play. I didn't have lines to learn, didn't have to be on the stage, and didn't have to wear anything unflattering. I was lucky enough to be the prompt and sat out of view for the entire event. Just the way I liked it.

During 1969 at the Girl Guides we had a celebration of 'Thinking Day', where we attended a camp fire for the patrol leaders at Blake Hall. We also had our photograph taken as a troop. This had never happened before. It was one of the very few activities where girls of every year took part. Other activities and clubs were either for specific years or attracted specific years.

Some clubs I just couldn't see the point of, such as Stamp Club. The members swapped and sorted stamps and visited other stamp clubs that did the same.

Wildlife Club sounded interesting, but I thought, like the sailing and seamanship club, it could only lead me into trouble. I've always been passionate about wildlife, but common sense told me that the wildlife in Essex was going to be rather small, and what I really liked was cats, very big cats. In any case I spent quite a bit of time trying to revise for exams.

I most liked the annual speech competition. I liked to read out aloud the set piece of poetry and give a five-minute speech on a topic picked from the list. I was encouraged to do this by the English teacher, who said that if I practised I would be fine. She listened to me and gave me advice on pronunciation of words that I was unfamiliar with, one such word being 'lugubrious'. I must have asked her every day for a week to remind me how to say that word! I never came first, but did manage to secure a placing and was chosen to represent my year by giving a reading at the School Carol Concert, which was a great honour. It went very well and I was really pleased. To be fair though, I had spent so much time at church that I had learnt the readings by heart, so I rarely even had to look at the reading, just say it. Every year I took part and some of the years it was disastrous as I had forgotten entirely what I was going to say or had stage fright, but the very last one was good, which only goes to show that if you stick at it and try, you do sometimes get a good result.

All I can say about House results is that I was always willing to give things a go. Like others I wasn't especially good at anything, but I was fairly enthusiastic and optimistic before events. At least, unlike my previous school, I was included, and the days of sitting on a bench hoping to be chosen were almost forgotten.

Mid-term weekends and absence from school

Half way through the term, pupils could have a weekend at home. Most of the 234 children went home, but there were always a few left at school. These were sometimes children from overseas whose families were in the Army, or those that lived too far away to be able to travel to and from home in a weekend to make it worthwhile.

It was thrilling for some to go home, and especially those who suffered from homesickness. It was something that was often looked forward to with mounting excitement, and there was a real buzz about the home weekend. There were different reasons for this. It could just be the change of routine, like being able to lie in bed for as long as you wanted, ride your horse, see your pet, go shopping, see siblings or meet up with a boyfriend, or something simple, like having different food to eat.

Probably one of the best things about a home weekend, whether you went home or stayed, was the fact that it was one less afternoon of lessons, as children went home after lunch on Friday. At the start of every year we always spent time looking at the timetable to see what was scheduled for Friday afternoon, hoping it wasn't Art, PE or Needlework. If it was double History or French it was double jubilation. If you were in the last year and it was a private study period, you felt robbed of what would have been a good end to the week.

It started off by packing your very small bag after the morning lessons, with some better-prepared girls packing theirs after breakfast, but these were few. I don't think much thought went into what was going home apart from dirty laundry, which your parents always seemed to be able to wash and iron without using copious amounts of starch, unlike the school laundry. It really was the only weekend that guaranteed for girls that your battleship greys wouldn't stand up of their own accord. If you were lucky like me and had a Nan who had friends that worked in a big London laundry, you could also have your blazer dry cleaned and all looking spick and span for the return to school on Sunday.

It all started with a pretty odd ritual. You had to go to the dining room with your weekend bag and wait until your parents had snaked around the school buildings, creating petrol fumes, in order to pick you up. The pickups were meant to be staggered, but of course we all used to tell parents to get there early in order to start our weekend. Not only that, but if a parent had two children in school, the youngest would be on a first pickup, which enabled the older sibling to escape at the same time. You just hoped that the cars in front of your parents didn't want to engage any of the teaching staff in conversation or argument. There were a few arguments about parents who thought they had been clever by queue jumping. They were often kept waiting and had to park adjacent to the pick-up point.

The queue started from the far end of the school and came along a long drive up to the side of the Art room, where there was a sharp right-hand turn, then a left, to wait outside the dining room. Some parents knew how to avoid this queue by taking another turning at the top of the drive and then cut in to the queue by squeezing in. Matron used to get so annoyed at parents who sped past Sick Bay to push in.

In the dining room a teacher would call out the names of the first four to be picked up and so on until the queue dwindled and the pupils left were conspicuous by the absence of everyone else. I was often last. This was really down to the fact that my Dad sometimes forgot the route and he and my Mum ended up somewhere unrecognisable in North Essex. My Mum was not a good map reader and had little sense of direction, and my Dad had little in the way of patience, so invariably it ended up, according to my Mum, with her throwing the map down and telling him that if he was so clever he should find the way himself. Even after five years the same thing happened time and time again. Mum said it wasn't her fault if people kept changing the scenery en route by building new things and changing the layouts.

It was however, without many good roads, quite a distance between Walthamstow and North Essex. My parents left my brother at home being looked after by Nan, because they used to give a lift to another girl who was in the year below me. Her Dad reciprocated by taking me on the return journey. I hated this because he had an unstable-three wheeler and it used to frighten the life out of me. Not only this, but we had to drive the whole journey with our luggage on our lap and without seat-belts. I hated the shared arrangement so much that sometimes I used to stay with one of my friends who lived in Epsom for the weekend. I liked the girl I went home with very much, but not the scary journey.

This arrangement only worked for three years, because then we moved to South Benfleet in Essex and my brother joined the school too. The same sort of arrangement applied on the way back, but parents could park up and walk back to your dormitory with you to help you with luggage; not that there was much in the way of clothes, but tuck came in big tins and that had to be delivered safely. It was, in my case, a full-size fruit cake to share with friends and swap for sweets in the early days of school. Later it was bottles of fizzy pop. For some strange reason, which might have been that we had plenty of energy to burn, we had a craze for Lucozade.

However, when I reached the fifth year it became records, my luggage consisted of toiletries, writing materials and extra books. I had grown out of sweets by the age of 14. They had been replaced by other luxuries, such as hair lacquer, tights and a camera. Musical instruments were transported to and fro as well, despite the fact that nobody ever practised their instrument at home.

We had to be back in school in time for tea on Sunday. We were full of stories about what we had been doing over the weekend; for many it meant having our hair cut, shopping for new casual clothes and visiting relatives, and for some it was a chance to meet their new brothers and sisters or see their pets. Some went to the cinema.

I loved seeing my cat, Dinky (she had a collar with a very small bell in pink), and my dog Sally, who was very pleased to see me home as it meant extra walks for her. After we moved, I also had the opportunity to explore Southend-on-Sea, walk down the pier and go on the beach, things I hadn't been able to do when living in London.

Moving also meant we were nearer to some of my mother's elderly relatives, all of whom had to be visited every time I was home. I missed all the familiar places and my old friends from Walthamstow and it felt lonely. Living in London I was used to regular public transport and could find my way around easily, but after moving this was problematic because I was unfamiliar with places and names and I only went out with my parents. Up until this time I had been completely independent. Childhood seemed to have come to an abrupt halt and I was thrown into adulthood, expected to sit and talk with relatives, most of whom had aliments which they talked about incessantly. It was no wonder I built up an extensive knowledge of osteo and rheumatoid arthritis. My cousin, who is a few years older than me, was at university studying medicine, and even he was impressed at how much I knew at fifteen, what with the family complaining about their ailments and two parents who filled the knowledge gap.

For some completely inexplicable reason my family also thought that I would love to visit Pitsea Market in the rain on a Saturday morning, to spend hours rummaging amongst kitchen paraphernalia, linen and odds and ends, in charge of the basket on wheels. I didn't.

There was nobody of the same age around. I couldn't wait to get back to school, and after the first trip to my new home I decided to stay for weekends from then on.

I had some extra trips to my Nan's house because I was having my teeth fixed in Harley Street by an orthodontist. I would have said 'straightened', but it involved much more than just wearing braces. Not only did I have wires on my teeth, with a little key to adjust them each week, but for more than two years I also had speech exercises. My jaw was not aligned correctly. After the really bad dentist episode my Nan decided that I should be accompanied to get my teeth fixed. I enjoyed these trips because I stayed with Nan, went to Harley Street with her and then we stopped at a coffee shop on the way back. This probably accounts for why I never seemed to appear in school photographs - it was usually one of my absence days on a Friday. My teeth were straighter by mid-way through the Fourth Form.

I told school that my parents were busy and couldn't pick me up for the visiting weekend, and told my parents I wanted to do extra study at school. It wasn't compulsory to have an excuse to stay, but it just seemed to satisfy each party. Matron took all those who stayed at school for the weekend into Sick Bay for the two nights, so that we could all be together and not on our own in a big dormitory. During the last year I had my own room and was allowed to stay in it for the visiting weekend. I was fine with my own company, but often I had a friend who stayed as well, and we would sign out and go for very long walks on those weekends. We also had the television to ourselves and if we stayed in Sick Bay, Matron used to let us stay up late and watch her television. Things were very casual for the few that stayed the weekend and we could more or less do whatever we wanted. I used to spend quite a lot of the time swimming, which was semi-supervised, in so much as you had to tell someone that you were going to the pool - that was it. No health and safety or nannying in the sixties!

I remember two of the weekends I stayed. The first was a most beautiful summer weekend with long hot evenings. I remember swimming, sunbathing and then sitting in the field after supper until sunset, making daisy chains and talking to a friend and a couple of teachers. I vividly remember the smell of dew in the early morning. I loved the way the sun shone across the field and appreciated the tranquillity, with only birdsong to keep you company. We stayed up well past our usual bedtime and because there were mixed ages staying the weekend, bedtime was the latest, at 10 pm.

The second weekend was just the opposite. It snowed heavily on the Friday and I remember sitting on a big radiator in the Common Room with my overcoat and a scarf on and still feeling freezing cold. There had been a lot of snow and it just wasn't possible to go out anywhere at all. That became a long weekend, because school decided to phone parents and tell them not to return to school on the Sunday but to stay indoors until things improved. I think I was at school for almost a week with very few others. This was going well until we lost our electricity supply, at which point I wished I was at home! Matron insisted that we wear our wellingtons with thick socks and not shoes, so my feet froze. I think it must have been one of the few times I wore my school scarf all day. One of the boys taught us how to play canasta, Newmarket and rummy, all in the space of three days. We played table tennis to keep warm, but never won a game against the boys. We had all our meals delivered to Sick Bay as the dining room was so cold. The tuck shop wasn't open, so we were allowed to go in the back door and help ourselves and just leave the correct amount of money for whatever we had taken. It was accurate to the penny.

We also used to get mountains of food at the staying weekends and everything that we considered favourite was on the menu.

The only other time I was absent from school was a second flu epidemic, when I was sent home on a Friday and had to spend three weeks at home until I had completely recovered. In that period too my own GP attacked the verrucas to such an extent that I would swear he was going to teach the visiting school doctor a lesson on how to eradicate them. However, despite his enthusiasm, he failed.

Expeditions

School Geography Trip: On the 26th October 1969, we headed off in the bright sunshine to Sussex for our school Geography trip. The good weather stayed with us for the duration of our four-day trip. We made the excursion in our old school van and stayed at a Youth Hostel in Patcham, near Brighton.

The old school van, driven by Mr Fogg, had two rows of seats opposite each other running the length of it. We sat opposite one another and laughed and joked throughout the journey. Despite a few feeling a bit sick, nobody was. It was a life experience to travel that far in a school van. It was noisy, uncomfortable and felt dangerous, as there were no seat belts in those days. It was also very crowded. There seemed to be quite a lot of discussion as to whether we would actually make it to Brighton or not. The teachers took the notoriously travel-sick pupils in their cars.

We left Essex, went through Kent and into Sussex, stopping at various places on the way. I can't remember much of the detail, apart for being told about the Cinque

Ports, which were over a thousand years old and were significant for military and trade purposes, the chalky South Downs being well drained and mostly used for arable farming, and a lot about the River Cuckmere. We went to a very windy Beachy Head, where you could hardly stand up. We were being told something, but never knew what it was, as we couldn't hear because of the wind. I never cared that much either, as just being outdoors was enough to make me happy.

On the first day we went to the valley of the River Cuckmere I remember being told that the lower part of its course is in the floodplain and it meanders, a well-known feature of the area. It flows fast through the chalk landscape of the South Downs of East Sussex and ends its journey in the English Channel. For some reason I did vividly remember that it has an oxbow lake, a U-shaped body of water formed when a wide meander from the main stem of a river is cut off to create a lake. Last year I reminded one of my school friends of this and she said 'oh yes, I remember that trip and the oxbow lakes'. For some reason we all remember the oxbow lakes and can say we have at least seen one.

On one of the days, we studied Lewes, being a gap town, and went to a cement works. Both seemed very exciting. Imagine finding a cement works exciting!

On another day we went to Newhaven Docks. I remember that the ferries went from Newhaven to Dieppe.

The last day we were split into two groups and then dumped somewhere in the middle of the South Downs with a map and given a point to rendezvous with the staff and the school van. The staff had been in the local pub, whilst we had sampled the gastronomic delights of pre-packed, soggy sandwiches and unboiled eggs. The eggs were unboiled because one of our team couldn't follow instructions on how to cook them. I remember when the first person tried to crack their egg and got in a mess he said 'oh I must have misinterpreted the cook's instructions'. The eggs had barely been shown boiling water, let alone hard boiled. There seemed to be quite a lot of discussion about asking a boy to cook eggs. We all thought he had purposely done it, so as not to be asked a second time. Despite this we were still happy and even more so at being on our own unsupervised.

Unknown to us, exactly the same adventure awaited us in the afternoon, but this time we were driven to a sandstone ridge in Ashdown Forest, where the staff waited for our return to a triangulation point. It was a good job one of our group had been paying attention and knew what a triangulation point was, as most of us didn't. As usual we were all mucking about and acting silly en masse when we met a lady who was obviously frightened by our behaviour and told one of our group not to come any closer as her poodle was dangerous. We all fell about laughing. It just goes to prove that being intimidated by young people is nothing new.

When we arrived at the meeting point, there was one teacher who, due to the lack of toilet facilities, had wet feet, but he was chanting 'Sandstone is impervious'. Somehow we seemed to find this hilarious and together with the poodle incident it kept us in high spirits.

One evening we all walked a rather long way to an off-licence, a place we had seen whilst we were returning to the hostel the previous evening in the school bus, to purchase cider. However we had to drink the whole lot before returning to the Youth Hostel, as alcohol was forbidden on the premises. By the time we returned, it was pretty obvious where we had been and what we had been up to. Nobody said a word about it to us, but we were told that the following evening we were not allowed to go out.

Whilst we were staying at the hostel we nicknamed the warden 'Mr Nasty'. He became our non-geographical entertainment throughout the period. We later found out he was the Assistant Warden. To satisfy himself that he was fulfilling his duties properly whilst the Warden was away, he inspected everything we were meant to do and at one point he demonstrated how to sweep a floor. I remember one from our party imitating him and everyone fell about laughing. We were laughing so much that after five years at boarding school the one thing we knew how to do to perfection was sweep a floor, having had five years of practice and the loss of house points until we got it right. In fact following his demonstration, we just had to put him right on his technique. There were only a few of us on this trip, but I remember it being very good fun.

The Royal Albert Hall

We had a trip to the Royal Albert Hall to listen to a Benjamin

Britten concert with a lady who was American and had joined the school staff to gain experience of working in an English boarding school. On our return she started the first School Glee Club. I remember sitting quite high up and thinking that the sound was wonderful. I sat next to her and she treated me as if I was someone who knew something about music. In fact I knew very little, but I knew what I liked.

Trip to Orfordness instead of Whiteacres exchange

We were all getting excited about our planned visit as part of an exchange trip with a School in Lancashire called Whiteacres, where our previous Deputy Head had taken a post. However, about ten days before we were meant to go, Whiteacres had an epidemic of chicken pox and it was cancelled. We were dreadfully disappointed. There had only been a few of us going, about eight girls. I had been desperate to travel as far away as Lancashire. My Nan had been to Blackpool and had told me all about it. Clacton on Sea was the farthest north I had been.

Instead we were told that the whole year would get a trip to Orfordness. Somehow it just wasn't the same, a day trip in place of a week away. We got on a large coach; at least we had teachers that we all liked. We made our way to the coast and then had to walk from where the coach dropped us off at Thorpeness to Dunwich, passing the Sizewell Power Station. It was a very cold and miserable day and the only part of it I remember enjoying was paddling near Sizewell in warm water. It was a walk of about ten miles and we stopped to have our sandwiches at lunchtime, but the last few miles battling against the wind and drizzle were the worst part and we were very glad when we spotted the coach. It could have put me off walking for life, it was so wretched. Dunwich itself had been very interesting and the best part of the walk. We were told that most of the town was now beneath the sea, but we could still see some old parts during our walk.

It wasn't as nice as a trip to Lancashire might have been for two reasons. The first was that I had looked forward to the trip for at least six months, and the second was that a lot of the girls had boyfriends and they had walked off as twosomes, leaving just a very few of us to try and make the best of a bad windy and wet day. Really I would have been happier to stay at school. The only upside was that my Granddad had given me £2 10 shillings as spending money for my trip, and when it was cancelled I offered it back, but he told me to keep it to help with the big disappointment.

Fifth Form boys' bikes

We often had our own little local expeditions where we teamed up with a boy with a bike and then rendezvoused somewhere in the local village. With the girl sitting on the handlebars, ,we proceeded towards Willingale Spain, where we sat in a big field talking. This ritual included girls who did not have boyfriends as well as those who did. Some of the trip was quite frightening as we used to go at quite a speed along those country lanes and of course the bikes were unbalanced with two people. It did enable me to see quite a bit of the Countryside around Fyfield though.

Suffolk Park, Walthamstow, the street where I lived

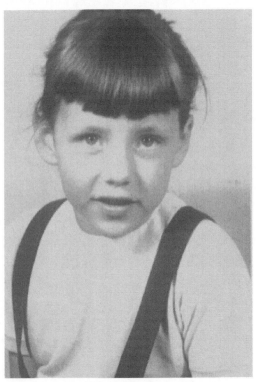

Diane at Stoneydown School

Stoneydown Park School

Stoneydown Park, next to the school

Walthamstow Library

St Michael's Church,
Walthamstow

Last week at Stoneydown School, 1965 –
Diane on the left in the striped top

Fyfield Open Air School

Fyfield School in 2001

The school from the air

View across the site

The new teaching block

Fyfield Staff with the Headmaster, Mr Underwood

Diane and brother Jeff in 1966

The quadrangle

The new dormitories

Mum outside the swimming pool at Fyfield

St Nicholas' Church, Fyfield

Inside St Nicholas' Church

Class 3A, 1968

At Fete Day, 1969

Diane and Jeff, 1970

Last week at Fyfield, 1970

Angela and Diane, 40 years after leaving Fyfield

Chapter Six

THE SCHOOL DINING ROOM, AND SOME UNUSUAL EXPERIMENTS

Eggy bread is now referred to as French toast, but if you asked anyone who went to Fyfield what was their favourite food, that's what most of them would say. It was one of our favourite breakfasts, usually served with boiled tinned plum tomatoes or baked beans. It was cooked by just soaking bread in beaten egg and deep frying it. It became in my time at school a Fyfield tradition that carried on throughout the years and is still requested at every school reunion, despite the fact that we are all a lot older now.

Another breakfast tradition was eating fried bread with marmalade or jam. Often sausages were eaten with marmalade too. These traditions remained in the school, as I still see pupils who left well after I did talking about these strange food combinations. I can't really account for how this all started except that if one person did it, another might try and before you knew it, we had a unique food experience!

Until I went away to school I ate cornflakes or toast, but at Fyfield I grew up thinking that cooked breakfast was a normal part of life. I don't think anybody had discovered healthy eating in the 1960s. We always started the day with a big breakfast, cereal or porridge, cooked, then toast and jam. And lots of it.

I am sure there have been many schoolchildren who dislike school food, but the food at Fyfield was good, very good. As we had breakfast, lunch, tea and supper at school, you had to learn to like it, but that was not difficult because of the variation in meals. If you came from a family that had little money, the food almost seemed exotic, and it allowed you to try dishes you had never eaten before. It was the first time in my life I had eaten cake, apart from at Christmas or birthday.

In 1967 tea became optional for the whole school. It was always bread and jam followed by cake, mainly Swiss roll. Pupils began to tire of the routine, so following a suggestion from the School Council that tea should become optional it was trialled and found to be successful, and that's the way it stayed. A late evening hot drink was extended in 1969 to all fifth formers, where previously it had been just for prefects. It was inclusive and it had been a decision made by the prefects at a School Council meeting, of which I was one.

One privilege of being a prefect was that if there was only one teacher eating at the teacher's table you could be invited to sit with him or her. Why this was considered a privilege I never knew; to me it was an ordeal, as I never knew what to talk about. That is except for one occasion, when the art teacher invited me and we talked about cars, mainly his car. I loved cars and still do.

Another School Council suggestion was to try curry. It was a fairly new and popular introduction to the UK. It was not part of the school menu, but the head cook was always very willing to listen to suggestions and then try to accommodate them. The curry was a huge success and often appeared on the menu. This was before curry became a popular food on the high street. There were not that many curry restaurants, especially outside London and other large cities at this time, so really Fyfield was leading the way with its exotic menu.

Among other food favourites were Friday fish and chips, steak and kidney pie, which was delicious, dumplings, which were scrumptious, and a most wonderful, spoon-breaking chocolate pudding, referred to as 'chocolate slab' and usually served with dark pink raspberry custard. A spoon and fork were needed in order to devour puddings and a good job too, as the fork had to be placed strategically on the chocolate slab before pounding the end of it with the spoon, with the ultimate aim of being able to break the slab without it jumping off the plate or splattering someone's uniform. After five years the art of slab pounding had been successfully mastered. First-formers never really got to grips with this pudding, so we usually ate theirs to relieve them of the embarrassment of trying to cope with it.

There were lots of other goodies too: steamed jam or syrup sponge pudding, spotted dick, cabinet pudding and pineapple upside-down pudding with cherries . Really there was nothing better on a cold winter day than ambling into the steamed-up dining room with the smell of pudding and custard wafting around.

It was rare that we ever had salad to eat as a main course, but we had a fair amount of cabbage and carrots as our main vegetable intake.

In 1969 we were allowed to cook our own toast, where previously we had it delivered on toast racks, which really meant that it was always cold by the time you ate it. This was a big improvement. We must now be the know-alls in hotels who instruct everyone else on how to use the toasting machines. It went onto a conveyor belt and came out the other end toasted.

Pupils usually fell into either loving or hating porridge; there didn't seem to be any middle ground. It was quite creamy, never lumpy and when sprinkled with lashings of brown Demerara sugar it was lovely and crunchy. It did though have a sinister luminous look, which put quite a few fussy people off trying it.

About once or twice a year we were treated to ice cream at supper time, usually accompanying jelly. There used to be quite a lot of excitement surrounding this event and it often got a mention in a letter to home. It was usually vanilla flavour, but once I remember it was Neapolitan, green, pink and brown. There seemed to be lots of discussion about the various flavours and swapping of colours. In those days even raspberry ripple was considered glamorous. It did seem strange that 'ice cream' was announced at morning messages. That is how important it was! It meant that it was going to be a hot and sunny day, and with ice cream at the end of it we kept extra cheerful all day long, as it was a highly-appreciated treat.

In the dining room, there were eight people to a table, three either side and one at each end. One person, referred to as a server, collected the food for the table for a day and cleared away every meal, taking the dirty plates to a hatch where the kitchen staff loaded huge dishwashers. This carried on throughout school life, with the exception of one period when the kitchen staff took industrial action. A rota of fourth and fifth formers then took it in turns to do 'kitchen duties' and as a reward were served extra portions of food after meals were over in the dining hall. We had our meal in a little wooden shack at the back of the dining hall. Obviously little attention was really paid to health and safety in those days as prefects in the fifth form job was to load, run and empty the steaming dishwashers at the hatch, unsupervised. This is where I learnt the art of wet tea towel flicking, hastily taught to us by the boys and perfected by the girls!

I did learn the phrase *'buenas noches, hasta mañana',* because the kitchen staff, very politely said this to all the servers when plates were taken to the hatch at suppertime. It was lovely and reminded me of home, where everyone spoke in their own language and got by in English and slang. An example of this was when my aunty used to say to me 'Ain't you no very hungry angelo'.

Dining room arrangements were also different when we were prefects too, as we sat at two tables of six at either end of the dining hall. The boys did most of the serving and carried empty plates, relieving the girls of this duty, as it was considered jolly good manners. It also impressed potential girlfriends, especially when they returned with a very heavy tray balanced on one hand.

Another unusual event occurred in the 1960s; the famous orange experiment. A researcher asked everybody to take part in a trial where a third of pupils drank a sieved orange juice drink that was a very watery squash, another third drank thick concentrated orange pulp, which was the whole inside of an orange pulped, and the remaining third ate a whole fresh orange. Being in the whole orange group had the advantage of making us the fastest orange peelers of today! I don't know how the researchers took account though of food swaps, where the orange was swapped for next morning's sausages. I was a lover of the big oranges, but really disliked sausages! It was called the 'vitaminised orange experiment', but I later learnt that oranges had vitamin A, B1, B2, B6, C, and E in anyway, so I wondered what they had been vitaminised with! Despite taking part in this experiment, I don't think we were ever party to the outcome or even in fact if there was one. The one thing this taught me which was useful in later life was that if you fail to monitor an experiment properly you cannot rely on the result. So the researcher might not have got what he wanted out of it, but I did.

Pupils were not allowed to arrive late for meals. They were told that the kitchen tried to get meals served on time, so it was polite to arrive on time to eat them. Punishment for arriving late for breakfast was the worst, walking around the dining hall three times, but it might also mean that you missed the eggy bread. Nobody was late for lunch as the dining hall was adjacent to the school block and after a morning's work, we were famished. There was little reason to be late, and as pupils valued their free time, if lunch finished promptly, it left a few minutes before either afternoon lessons or more signing-out time if we were on winter timetable. If pupils were late for supper, then half-hour prep was usually added. This deterred us from being late; again the half an hour or so free time was valuable.

In 1970 a girl in our year called Carole conducted a poll and the question asked was, 'Do you think school food is of a good standard?' Only 29% said no. Looking on the positive side, 71% were happy. I am sure I did not appreciate the complexities of getting meals cooked and ready to serve on time. From a personal perspective, my family were not well off and couldn't afford a whole array of food, so there were some things I had for the first time at school, eggy bread being one of them. Puddings were another. Occasionally I ate tinned fruit and at Christmas, trifle. I had not eaten a whole array of vegetables, mostly runner beans and peas, because everyone in London grew them in their garden. I was introduced to cabbage, cauliflower, cucumber and radishes.

So school did a lot to improve my palate and gave me confidence to choose and eat a wide variety of food in restaurants after leaving school. However cake, biscuits and puddings were no longer part of my diet after school. Maybe it was a London thing or an adult thing; we had a main meal and occasionally an apple, but not pudding or cake unless it was a special event.

The school dining room was like a window onto the school world. It had a certain buzz to it. It was noisy and happy and reminded you of the constant business of the school. You could see all the comings and goings of staff and visitors. You could talk to those who sat around you but were not in your house or classes. It was one of the times I saw my brother, because despite being at the same school, funnily enough we didn't actually see that much of one another at all.

Subjects and lessons

Considering there were so few pupils at the school, a wide range of subjects was taught. However, subjects in the 1960s were still assigned to gender. There were traditionally Domestic Science and Needlework for girls and Woodwork and Metalwork for the boys. This was because society hadn't yet fully moved forward to accepting that girls could become engineers or boys could become secretaries. There were of course a few who did and things were slowly changing, but generally speaking school leavers went into careers, such as nursing, secretarial or hairdressing for girls and the police force, farming and motor mechanics for boys. It was also more likely that boys would go on to take A levels and have a university education at the end of the 1960s.

A general gripe among some of the girls was that Fyfield did not teach shorthand and typing, which was a very popular subject among girls generally during the 60s. Some of us were pleased that they didn't, because we had already decided not to become secretaries. Fyfield had this effect on girls, who generally became very independently-minded and self-sufficient. A secretary was, to us, nothing more than a glorified office waitress, usually to a man, but this is how it appeared during the 60s and television reinforced it.

I did, however, learn a lot of office skills which were needed as a civil servant, so later I took a course in both shorthand and, typing which included using a sheet of carbon paper and flimsy paper to produce a file copy. In addition I learnt how to use Roneo and Gestetner duplicating machines and an electronic electrically-driven, 10-key add-lister, but that was primarily so I could build my office skills to enable me to move upward. When computers came into the Civil Service I adapted to the change very quickly and my skills were useful, particularly as I could touch-type by that time.

One of the more unusual subjects taught in the younger years at Fyfield was Rural Science, which is defined as 'the study and theory of agriculture, biology, ecology, and associated fields'. I say unusual, but from my research on Open Air Schools, it was generally on the curriculum. Rural Science at Fyfield took the nickname of 'rural digging' or 'double digging', being a double period of activity. There was no theory at all, and the closest we got to associated fields were the ones we escaped to on the boys' bikes!

The school had some plots, similar to allotments, where we had a double period of outside fresh air activity which was meant to teach us the rudiments of rural science, such as crop rotation. I only ever remember growing lettuce and radishes - very large radishes. Because nobody liked them they were just planted and watered and weeded for a whole season and grew bigger and bigger. My radishes ended up the size of pumpkins!

Our teacher, Polly as we called her, stood at the end of the plots with her hands on her hips bellowing all sorts of gardening tips. She was about as interested in rural science as we were and had about the same level of knowledge or less, because if you ever asked a question she told you that you could always look it up in the library and that's what libraries were for. We knew what the shed was for. It was for her to light her cigarettes out of the wind, and boy did we get an earful if we needed a garden implement just as she was lighting up!

We were just pleased to be outside rather than in, and I don't remember any of us taking a GCE or GCSE in Rural Science. On the plus side, I did learn how to use all the garden implements and on a lovely summer's day, it was a very welcome activity. It was occasionally competitive, as I remember one open day one of my classmates taking her mother and father to show them what she had grown and saying, 'of course my rows are a lot straighter than anyone

DIANE LANGDON

else's because I did it properly with the string'. We ribbed her about it for the whole of the following year. We used to wear our culottes or very tight shorts for this activity, which I remember pleased the boys. I don't actually remember the boys doing any of the gardening, other than standing there in order to tell us girls whether or not the rows were straight.

In the fifth form a spell of digging was often given as a punishment to boys in order to dampen their romantic ardour. One particular boy in my year must have dug that plot several times over for being caught with his girlfriend snogging in the drying room. We used to walk by the plots and say 'Oh hello, you've been caught again then?' He used to reply 'Well at least I know I'll never go into a career as a gardener'.

One chap who went to Fyfield recalls how in metalwork, he didn't remember wearing any protective clothing such as goggles, because you were told how to be safe and everyone sensibly obeyed the rules. Health and safety was not really imposed on us during the 1960s, we were just told what was sensible for our own good and most were responsible students who listened. There were one or two accidents, but no more than you would expect nowadays for all the health and safety laws. Not that I am against health and safety law, but I think if there are too many guidelines, common sense seems to disappear because people become used to being told what to do instead of thinking for themselves.

In Domestic Science there was the very nasty accident of the exploding Scotch egg during our exam, which shook us all. An air bubble had got trapped between the egg and sausage meat and when the girl put it into the really hot boiling oil, it went bang and exploded in a most extraordinary manner, showering her with fat. She was taken to hospital and the rest of us had to try and carry on. Not that it made much difference to me, as I knew I was going to get a poor mark - nothing much to do with my ability, just my attitude apparently.

Domestic Science was excellent when we cooked, but I hated it when we had to study how to launder different fabrics. We also had meal planning sessions, where we studied food groups and vitamins in very great depth. The cookery sessions seemed to be few and far between, although we did enjoy sitting in the nice bright and airy Domestic Science room on stools and getting to use the washing machine.

There was also a good view of anyone playing sports in the Quadrangle, should you get bored. I often got bored and never really got to grips with meal planning, as my philosophy was to eat whatever you liked or fancied. I played the meal-planning game but vowed never to actually use it in life. My take on it was that if everyone used it, how come very few had good figures and why was it that a lot of the adults were out of breath climbing the simplest of inclines? The vitamin and minerals section I was well attuned to, as this helped with my Human Biology studies, which I much preferred.

My grasp on laundry was thus: it was divided into two main groups. It was either clean (but needed refreshing) or dirty, and it was as simple as that. All the label gazing was well beyond my attention span.

However, the teacher decided that I would wash her smalls in the twin tub as part of my education at the same time as making pancakes. This was a big mistake. All was going well and that week I had the washing task combined with the pancake-making, so the twin tub was adjacent to my stove. As you can imagine, we got to the point of tossing the pancake, when oops! My pancake disappeared into the twin tub and quickly became a glutinous mess, sticking to the Aertex vest and rather large panties. How anyone could call them smalls I never knew! I just couldn't help myself, but I fell about laughing and nearly choked when the teacher accused me of being lazy and not bothering to make a pancake. Not only that, I tried to advise her on the dangers of using a machine full of water close to an electric cooker, and only name-dropped Matron when talking about what could happen when you were careless with water near electricity. She took my arm, removed my apron and I was taken outside. Every time I looked at her face I laughed, and the harder I tried to suppress the laughter the more the giggles took a grip on me. I laughed until it really hurt.

I was marched over to the boys' room, where woodwork theory was in progress. She opened the door and said to the teacher, 'Can you take this disobedient and unruly child? She doesn't deserve to learn how to cook'. He told me sternly to sit at a spare bench and carried on with the lesson. Then he came over to me and asked what had happened and I recounted the story in half sentences amid snorts of laughter. The whole of the boys' class were hooting with laughter and making jokes and the teacher was trying very hard not to laugh too, but he was laughing so much that he had to turn his back on me to compose himself and I could see his shoulders shaking.

I had three weeks of technical drawing and woodwork, as he thought the situation should be given time to calm down. I was very grateful, as I found I just loved the drawing instead of menu planning and laundry, not to mention the hardship of being in a class full of sixteen-year-old boys.

On my return to the Domestic Science class the woodwork teacher's advice was to try to act humble and sorry, even if I wasn't, so it was pretty evident that the other side of the story had been given to whoever had been in the staff room. I knew this as a male teacher had teased me in lessons by saying 'Ah yes, next lesson it's Domestic Science for the girls, and Diane, try not to cook up a storm this week'.

Geography was also a very popular subject, once again because it involved trips away from school and out in the fresh air. In our particular year we visited the South Downs, staying in a Youth Hostel and visiting the Ashdown Forest. I always remember a teacher telling us that sandstone was impervious. We had already assumed this, because we had noticed his wet shoes and a puddle where he had obviously been caught short whilst waiting for us to return to the school van. From that day on, every time we had a geography lesson, one of the boys would ask, 'Is that impermeable, sir?' every single time any sort of rock was mentioned in class.

Needlework was also a disaster for me. I spent an inordinate amount of time cutting out a pattern, only to find after sewing it to find that the material was attached to my school jumper. The teacher despaired of my lack of needlework skills, but secretly she must have had a good laugh at my expense, as I know my classmates did. Despite this, she never gave up and had enormous patience, which was common to most of the teaching and ancillary staff. Luckily a distant aunt of mine got a job as a seamstress at the school and I was able to wander along to her little room in the middle of the quadrangle to get expert advice. She was always pleased to see me and often saved me her morning chocolate biscuits. She never did anything for me, but she used to say, 'Well you just need to tack this to here and then bring it back for me to see'. From then on my needlework improved. She also taught me to knit.

Mathematics was one of my favourite subjects, particularly geometry, because I could understand the logic of it and remember most of the theorems. I was in the top set for mathematics, with only one other girl and lots of boys. The boys were very supportive and would help you out when you were stuck with a problem, wanting to show you just how easy problem-solving was. Twelve years after leaving school, I took a GCE in Maths and another in Modern Maths and Accounts at both O and A level, so some of the teaching must have been worthwhile, despite the fact that it took a while before I developed confidence in the subject. People often say they can't understand why they had to learn obscure maths, particularly algebra, which they have never used in their lives, but I could see the use of this subject as it developed analytical skills which I put to use later on.

Sport featured very highly in school. There were so many sports to choose from that it was unlikely that you couldn't find a sport to try. Athletics and rounders were high on the list of girls' team sports in the summer and hockey during the winter. Badminton and tennis were minority sports, but still encouraged, and I became a fairly accomplished player of both. The school had its own swimming pool, which thanks to a group of parents was covered in during my second year there, so swimming was a regular activity. I used to go to recreational swimming about three to four times a week. We also had a swimming gala once a year, held at the Harlow Pool, where each house competed and the Fifth Form pupils devised an amusing and witty event at the end of the evening which included all of them.

During the last two years of school a new teacher of English joined who introduced the pupils to Film Studies (called Additional English Studies), which immediately became a popular subject. We examined propaganda, advertising and themed films. Our English lessons also took on a different format whereby we did less formal essay writing and carried out more group analysis activity. This was the first time lessons had been like this and it enabled us to understand more about each other's opinions. The

Fourth Form Additional English Studies group also helped to produce the first Fyfield School Magazine, which had previously been known as the Clatterford Chronicle. Every form in the school contributed to it in some way, and the results of the latest pupil survey also formed part of it.

Private study sessions were a time when we had a free period, so we could study anything we wanted. This generally involved a lot of discussion about fashion and music among the girls. When you reached the fifth year it also included serious study of film stars and boys.

I loved Art too, not that I was any good at it at school, but later I went on to take courses in oil painting which I really enjoyed. I loved everything about Art, the smell of the room, the airiness of the room, the teacher, who never seemed to get impatient with anyone, and the ease of the lessons. I think this was the lesson I looked forward to the most.

I won't say too much about the sciences, except they involved an awful lot of experiments and not much else until pre-exam time. It was handy to get those Bunsen burners activated on a cold winter's morning though! I won't say anything about explosions either, except that they did increase the numbers of students that took sciences the following year.

Now you must be wondering whether or not I actually was good at anything and what I liked. Well I liked Art, Biology, Human Biology, Geography and Mathematics. I also enjoyed Social History.

I obtained the best results in English, Additional English and Geography before leaving school, but after school I discovered some subjects I liked a lot more, such as Modern Mathematics and Accounts. I also enjoyed written French, which I studied at night class for two years.

Writing letters home

Writing letters home once a week was compulsory, and if, like some of us, you had seen your parents at the weekend because they had been to the school for Open Day, carol concert or the like, you had to write a letter to someone else, such as a grandparent or aunt. So we sat at our desks with a pen and one piece of lined paper and a stamped envelope every Sunday evening. As soon as the letter was written we put our hands up. A monitor or teacher came to have a quick glance at it and if there was enough content, then the rest of the time was free. It was obvious really that letter-writing became quicker and quicker, until in the last year it was accomplished in well under five minutes. Sometimes we wrote things of interest in a rough book, so that when it got to Sunday we had something to remind us.

None of us had any letter-writing experience because we hadn't ever been anywhere. In the beginning we said to teachers, well what do you have to put in a letter?

It was suggested that every letter should start the same: *Dear Mum and Dad, I hope you are keeping well. With love from...* In the first year this was about as much as the parents could expect. In the second year, it had developed and went *Dear Mum and Dad , I hope you are keeping very well. PS Please send some money, even sixpence will do. Yours desperately...*

By the third year, far more was expected of us. To my amazement I found I was quite an accomplished letter writer and I could fill my week by writing many girls' letters home for a very small fee. To be safe though, I insisted that they should read them before they were sent, just in case they were caught out at a later date on the content. However, my letters seemed over time to develop very long and intricate passages, describing verruca treatment. I think parents were becoming suspicious to hear of an outbreak of verrucas in the school. Even Matron had commented that it did seem strange that so many parents had become obsessed with the latest verruca outbreak and wanted to talk to her about them every time they met her. That was a result of being sick bay monitor, nevertheless I took the hint!

I had to develop a better and more interesting strategy if my letter-writing skills were to remain productive. So I thought of a good idea, or so I thought at the time. I thought, what could be better than to start the letter off in the normal way, pop into the library, especially as I spent quite a bit of time in there anyway, get out a few books and read them, wait until I get to an interesting passage and copy it as the bulk of the letter? This only worked well for the first couple of weeks, but then I came unstuck, seriously unstuck. I had been reading a very good novel but had inadvertently in my rush to get the letter-writing job finished included an excerpt on drug-taking. Not only that but I had written it in two letters, one being to my own parents!

I found that both sets of parents had got in touch with

the Headmaster and asked him what was happening at the school and did he know about this drug-taking? It was after this that I had to come clean. The Headmaster made me promise that I should never do it again. I was tasked with finding something far more appropriate, but a little less enterprising, to do with my time. It was a shame, as my Nan had quite enjoyed the poetry of Rupert Brooke, thinking it was mine. I was never punished for it though! Not even the loss of one house point. It was explained and forgotten.

Later when my brother had a short spell at my school, which wasn't until my last year there, I had plenty of tales to tell. By this time though, I had been so unfairly tainted with having a fanciful imagination that my parents never believed anything I wrote. It was a shame, as everything was true and almost unbelievable too, including the day he acquired a cat's eye whilst out on a school trip. He was just intrigued by its composition.

The cat's eye is a retro-reflective safety device used in road marking. It consists of two pairs of reflective glass spheres set into a white rubber dome, mounted in a cast-iron housing. A key feature of the cat's eye is the flexible rubber dome, which is occasionally deformed by the passage of traffic. A fixed rubber wiper cleans the surface of the reflectors as they sink below the surface of the road (the base tends to hold water after a shower of rain, making this process even more efficient). The rubber dome is protected from impact damage by metal 'kerbs', which also give tactile and audible feedback for wandering drivers. Well, it did before my brother nicked it!

The second item was a tad more understandable, with him being a Sea Scout, although to be fair it caused a bit more of a rumpus. It was an anchor from a yacht. He had hidden it underneath his school blazer. This too was returned with a letter of sincere apology.

My brother! I was proud of him, because at least he was developing his own character and taking a bit of the spotlight away from me. His naughtiness made me seem good by comparison, which of course I wasn't.

I never knew why my brother felt compelled to acquire these items and it remained a mystery for many years until, in 2013, I met one of his classmates, who explained to me there was kudos in one's acquisitions made on a school trip - the bigger, the better! I had never realised this, as girls behaved differently.

For some inexplicable reason, writing had fashions. We were not allowed to use biro; it had to be proper ink. Then the 'girls' went through a phase of writing with spider-thin nibs, so the words almost cut into the paper. The last phase was proper italic writing with a proper italic wide nib, the wider the better. The ink that was fashionable I still use today, a turquoise blue.

I was trusted to supervise a class of letter writing when I was a prefect. I really enjoyed this, because it enabled me to advise the younger pupils what they should write about, but it was mainly what they had been doing, what we had to eat or anyone we had seen at school, nothing exciting really. I also used to write out a letter for my brother to copy to try and keep him out of trouble. I kept this to sports scores and walks in the countryside, interspersed with various items from the school menu. By this time I was the Head Librarian, so I was becoming far more responsible and slightly better behaved.

Quite a few years after leaving school, I wrote, by hand, a ministerial submission and then went to the Minister to talk about the content. The very first thing he said to me was that my handwriting was exquisite, and he asked me where I had learned to write so well. I met him in a work capacity several times and he always referred to me as the 'Fyfield gel with lovely handwriting'. How things have changed. Last week (2013) I went to observe the Scottish Parliament in action, and there was the Minister with her iPad in front of her, during a prisons debate.

To this day I still hand-write many letters as the computer doesn't really seem to me to have the same personal touch, but usually sticking to fact rather than fiction. Or maybe not.

Pocket money

The teachers each had accommodation in the vicinity of a dormitory. A teacher was responsible for the pupils in a particular dormitory or location. Each pupil deposited an amount of money with the teacher at the beginning of each term. Then they made an arrangement to pay pocket money on a certain night of the week, and unless you had a desperate expense, they kept to this routine. As far as I can remember this was usually some time on Friday evening before lights out, and it fitted nicely with the weekend and being able to spend money on the Saturday.

The way it operated was that one pupil went into the teacher's room and collected the amount they asked for, then each pupil went in as they saw the last coming out. There was no queuing system. Paying-out time was usually just a time frame of half an hour and if you missed it, it was your hard luck, you would have to wait until the following week, unless the teacher made an exception. Not everyone went each week. Sometimes you had money left from the week before, or if you had a weekend home, you usually returned with some extra pocket money.

The teacher kept a tin box with lots of change in it. We had halfpennies, pennies, threepenny ('thrupney') bits, sixpences, shillings, two shillings (florins) and two shillings and six pence, called a half crown. Mostly we liked having our pocket money in small denomination, such as shillings and sixpences. The shopkeeper in Fyfield Village Stores always moaned if a lot of us went into his shop with a half crown. In fact he moaned quite a lot about us going into his shop at all, and brought in a silly rule about only two pupils being allowed in at any one time, so we didn't crowd it out and scare other shoppers. So one day we went and stood outside his shop all afternoon and bought nothing! This had been the idea of one of the prefects, a boy known for his wit. We did it just to annoy him and then we went in, in threes rather than two, and two of us made out we didn't know the third. The third person wore a headscarf, hat or cap, but there was always some element of disguise to the act. To go with the disguise, there was also some pretty poor play-acting, like calling the third person 'Mrs Jones' or 'Farmer Elworthy'. Although to be fair we usually burst out laughing at something stupid one or other of us had said in these make-believe conversations.

The funniest conversations were when someone had looked up some medical information and then requested a shampoo and asked the shopkeeper whether or not it cured a whole range of ailments, to which the shopkeeper replied that if we wanted a shampoo for dandruff we would have to go to the chemist in Ongar. We never fooled anyone, not the shopkeeper or anybody who had been genuinely shopping. A couple of customers shook their heads or smiled. At one time I remember going into the shop with roller skates on. The shopkeeper got so exasperated that he phoned school and complained to the Headmaster.

That gave us the idea of opening our own tuck shop to make a profit to give to charity. The teacher marked the amount of pocket money taken in a book and you had to sign for however much you had withdrawn, and she would then write the balance underneath and ask you to check it. At the end of the term, they would do a final payout before the holidays when the whole balance was returned. Sometimes we felt really rich if we hadn't spent much money during the term.

Each term was around ten to twelve weeks long and each pupil paid in around £2. The upper limit on pocket money during the early years was about 2/6d a week, which in today's money equates to 12.5p, although I remember that towards the last year of school it had risen to 3/6d.

A lot of our money at aged eleven was spent on sweets,

with a Mars Bar, bigger than it is today, costing 6d or 2.5p today. The Picnic bar, described as more like a banquet than a picnic, was very popular because it was chewier and lasted a bit longer. The fairly dismal Aztec bar was introduced when I was at Fyfield and became a craze until we tired of it. You could buy Fruit Salad Chews, Black Jacks and Flying Saucers, four for one old penny. Lollies were between 4d and 6d, depending on the type. Sky Rocket was a first year favourite. Bubblegum was frowned upon, especially blowing it up until it burst. Gobstoppers were popular because they lasted the whole afternoon and were cheap to purchase. Chewing gum was banned. In the final year, girls generally did not buy sweets as they were considered childish.

The only other item I could remember spending my money on during those early school days was shampoo, which came in sachets and not bottles.

When I grew a bit older I was able to venture into Ongar, but it was a three-mile walk each way. Sometimes we had a school bus to take us one way. Usually we walked the other, but often on a Saturday we walked both ways. This provided the added advantage of being able to visit the bakery and buy a cake. My favourite was jam turnover or an iced bun. There was a chemist's shop which sold all sorts, and I remember in the latter years buying hair lacquer. There was also a very small haberdasher where you could buy buttons and a reel of cotton. Such a lot of cotton was needed to shorten those skirts and take in the side seams of shorts!

There was only one lasting memory I had regarding

pocket money, and that was when one of the teachers who held our money was engaged to be married. None of us knew who it was, but one pocket money evening we went in turn into her room and he was there to give us our money. He tormented each of us, saying 'Oh, I don't think you need as much as that. Do you?' Then we had to beg for more money. He was only teasing us. He also used to add the balance up wrong, just to test who really checked it. So we all knew who the fiancée was before the rest of the children at school, or we thought we did. Of course it wasn't a secret beyond breakfast the next morning! The boys told us that they had seen her visiting his room when they were supposed to be asleep. Of course from then on, we girls always wanted to get our pocket money from him.

In other years I remember not liking the teacher quite so much, so I rarely went to get pocket money, especially if I was asked what I was going to spend it on. I expect they were just trying to be friendly, but sometimes I just didn't know and if you said you didn't know, she used to ask whether it was really needed. I used to think it was bad enough being frugal with your own money, but someone else's?

We always put into the church collection on a Sunday and we donated money to sponsored walks and swims. We were quite attuned to charity and very aware of the plight of others.

We used to be very generous with one another in the Fifth Form, especially among the Prefects, lending or giving each other small change. We would also be kind to the first-formers who had 'run out of money' too early in the week, by giving them the odd sweet or two or a few odd pence. Sometimes if they were feeling homesick we would give them money for a call home. It was like belonging to a family where your brother or sister needed a bit of help.

Punishments, the field and essay writing

The school had a house point system and a black mark system. House points were deducted for minor offences and black marks for more severe misdemeanours. There were also punishments and expulsion.

Black marks were introduced only during my last year at Fyfield. I think it was because we had a change of Deputy Head and the new one wanted to instil more discipline into the school. Her slipper would become notorious in years to come. Until this time, if you had lost thirty or so house points that really was all that had happened and a small punishment was given. It was unfortunate, but there were a few forgetful pupils around who always seemed to be the ones who lost the house points. They were often very likeable pupils who had a bad memory or who just hadn't yet settled into school life. They were often the free spirits and the more interesting pupils. Conversely, those who never lost house points were not necessarily the most popular of pupils. Perhaps it was the burden of having to carry the 'good' reputation that made them seem less appealing.

We had a room set aside for those who would miss 'The Film' on a Saturday night, and who had instead a period of detention. It depended on who was taking the detention session as to the punishment, but most of them were written punishments, ranging from lines to creative writing. The French teacher gave the best detention. He said he never wanted lines as they were wasteful, but he gained a great deal of pleasure in reading essays produced during detention class. If they were not amusing or though-provoking, he would issue a further spell of detention. That was quite a challenge.

I only ever remember getting one detention during my whole time at school. I had forged my laundry list signature and signed it with a male film star's name. This was my personal protest against anyone having to check anyone else's dirty laundry and sign to say they had. I was told to write an essay titled 'Utter Exhaustion Defeats Sleep'. I think I wrote about ten pages and the teacher said 'All I can say Diane, is it is very different to what I was expecting and it's amusing so far', followed by 'Diane, this has sent me to sleep by the sixth page, so you may go as I haven't the energy to read any more'. This was just as well really, because by page eight I had written something really horrid about how his droning on about irregular French verbs had sent me to sleep during class two years previously and that was why I had taken History instead of French. Later I found out that he had in fact read it all! Every time I saw him I got teased a little bit more.

As for nicknames, he called me 'the second class road' (my surname was Broad - ie B road), and said I should think myself lucky, as I could at any stage be relegated to an unmade road or track. Heaven forbid I would become a footpath! He subsequently changed it to 'diamante', a play on Diane, which, he explained to me, was used for decorative purposes and not at all bright. He had a point. It could have been far worse, as others had greatly inferior nicknames. Generally the nicknames were amusing and not malicious. When he told me about diamante he saw that I had smiled and I understood it and was quite amused by it too. Lots of our nicknames were a play on our actual names. I am sure I used to play to my nickname as well at times. We were not meant to like our nicknames, we were meant to be a bit aggrieved or offended by them. I wasn't.

I regularly lost house points for talking after lights out, along with everyone else in the dormitory, but a couple of interesting things happened in each of the years I can recall. In the first year I was in a dormitory with a good friend, Angela. It was just impossible for us not to talk. Our dormitory was on one side of a quadrangle and it was called Clare 1 and looked out onto lovely open fields on the other aspect. Like Clares 2, 3 and 4 we had a small fire door leading to a quadrangle, which was always open. One night Angela started to act up and we were all laughing. I think she must have fancied herself as some sort of gymnast, as there she was swinging around on one of the very high pipes that went across the room, when a teacher came to ask what the noise was about. We said it must be because we had the windows open and noise from outside. Having accepted this she then proceeded to enquire where Angela was. It was quite funny as Angela was suspended in mid-air above her head, and how she never saw her we will never know. We said she had probably gone to the bathroom. This was at the other end of the dormitories and around the corner, quite a long way away. As soon as the teacher had gone to sort out some noise in the adjoining dormitory, Angela jumped down, went out through the fire door, did the quickest sprint you had ever seen, and pretended to rummage about in her boot locker for something.

During correspondence with Angela in 2009 she wrote to me:

I can remember swinging on those pipes that went through the top of Clare dorm and a teacher walking through after lights out - she didn't see me up there but someone told her I was in the locker room. My hands were really burning. We usually could only hold on briefly. I had to jump down - out the door into the quadrangle, into the other door, run down to the boot room and pretended I was looking for something in my locker - as she was checking every toilet cubicle. I don't know how I got away with it. Sure hurt my hands.

The second punishment I remember so well was again for talking after lights out en masse at gone 11pm. I suppose the Deputy Head, Polly, had just about had enough and as she told us, she had been in and warned us three times. On the fourth occasion, she said 'you are obviously not tired enough, so get up'. We had to get out of bed and put our mackintoshes on over our nightdresses and then put on our outdoor shoes. Without any knickers on it was definitely draughty. In the pitch black, she told us to follow her. She was the only person who had two torches, one in her pocket and one in her hand. She took us up to the school field, right to the very end of it, which was quite a way. We were all giggling and at this point she shouted, 'I am not very amused, you might be, but I'm not, so silence unless you want further punishment'. It went quiet.

I've never really known a night to be so very dark. Usually there is a moon or a little bit of light, but this night it was completely dark. She then said 'I am going to teach you to march' and with that we all stood in rows and had to swing our arms and keep in step, up and down up and down. When we had all got the hang of keeping in step and our arms swinging correctly with the step and how to change direction on command, she told us to stop. We thought we were going in, but she said 'Form a long line and you may then march around the perimeter of the field five times'.

It was now well gone midnight. She stood in the middle of the field with her torch shining on us as we swiftly marched around the field, until her batteries went dead. However, this episode was not without incident, because at one point she told me to lead the way at the front of the queue and when we turned a corner I put my arm out as an indicator of a turn, just like an old-fashioned car, and everyone fell about laughing. The girls behind me started to sing 'You put your left arm in, left arm out, in out, in out and shake it all about and do the hokey cokey, that's what it's all about'. Some of them did actually twizzle around when the hokey cokey part was sung. Personally I thought it was quite artistic and in complete time to the singing. Our music teacher would have been proud of the performance.

The Deputy Head came striding across to us and was so very cross, asking us if we thought it was amusing and one girl said well actually yes, it was extremely funny really. She said, 'Hands up all of you who thought it hilarious', and about half of us put our hands up. She said 'Right, you lot can go back to bed and you will be doing this again for another three nights!'

The following three nights were actually very nice, with plenty of moonlight and the smell of the grass that had been mown that day added to the pleasure of marching. We were also better prepared and grateful that those very large battleship-grey knickers would keep us so warm in the nether regions. We also filled our pockets with mints to help us concentrate during the expedition. Marching wasn't all that bad! I think the Deputy Head had an affinity with lively energetic and feisty girls. The excluded lacklustre non-participants languished in dormitories, having fun sleeping.

In 2010 one of my classmates said to me 'I can remember Polly standing in the middle of the field with her cigarette, and all we could see of her was a red dot jotting back and forwards. I have had that image in my head forever when I think of her.'

I managed to get through school without losing a black mark at all, but I don't really know how. Luck played a big part. I always seemed to be given the benefit of the doubt.

House points were lost for walking on a footpath at the back of the teaching block; this was for teachers and prefects only, being late for class or anything that required you to be on time; leaving PT or games kit in the school instead of taking back to your dormitory; leaving any property where is should not be; running when you should be walking; not cleaning shoes to the required standard; talking after lights out; and really anything else that just happened to irritate teachers or prefects. You soon learnt that there was no consistency about the losses either. So it was handy to work out quickly the moods of those who could deduct house points and keep out of their way. Personally, I kept well clear of the Domestic Science teacher in my last year as I think I would have been deducted a house point for just breathing. I would rather have taken a long detour than have to walk within a yard of her. I wasn't going to be caught out. From the washing machine episode on, she kept her eye on me.

House points were gained for doing things that were kind or thoughtful or for which you did not expect to get recognition, such as excellent work. Most weeks mine balanced out but as I got older they went into single figures per term - a very big achievement! I still lost four in the year I was a Prefect and meant to be setting a good example! They were for playing a prank on the maths teacher (that was not me personally, I was just in the class that did it and in fact it was the boys, not the girls), talking, more talking and further talking. In earlier years I got the hang of having to be very good and doings lots of good deeds to help balance out the losses, but by the fifth year I never bothered. I mean, what would have been the point?

In the early years I was just not used to the whole of a new school routine and lost most house points for forgetfulness, cheekiness and talking. Forgetfulness was because I was so busy getting from one activity to another that I mostly forgot about hockey boots needing to be cleaned or PE kit left in the changing room. Cheekiness was a good old East End defence mechanism that I had used previously to get myself out of scrapes. The trouble was I wasn't any longer in the East End and I didn't really have any need to be defensive. Talking was mostly after lights out and I just loved the fact that I had many friends and wanted to know all about them. There really weren't enough hours in the day! I've never really learned the art of keeping quiet. It's a terribly difficult skill to master.

The loss of thirty house points was converted into one black mark. Each week about three or four pupils fell into this category - they'd just had a bad week. In the last year, as we wanted the house point shield, we set up a system whereby the prefects checked that everyone from their house had picked up things from the teaching block and kept our eye on the few that contributed the most to house point losses, just to keep them in order and remind them constantly, and this enabled us to win the trophy most weeks. I don't know whether it could be considered cheating, but it did teach me the very useful art of co-operation to achieve a goal. The outcome was that we watched Top of the Pops on a Thursday evening for winning the shield.

During my time at Fyfield I never had any form of physical punishment. I was never caned or slippered. After my experiences at my previous school I was grateful for that. I don't think that form of punishment does ever achieve the desired effect anyway. The worst I endured was holding pillows out on each arm or remaking my bed several times and a few very jolly walking activities.

I do know of pupils who were slippered and caned for stealing. I think it would have been far better if someone had explained to them the consequences of their actions and made them apologise instead of hitting them. But I suppose there are only a few chances you can give people and it could not be just coincidence that one particular person always seemed to be punished. The Headmaster once summed it up, as I heard him say to someone when he was giving one of his good tellings-off, 'Your parents pay for you to be able to come to this school and they have to go without in order for that to happen, so you owe it to them to behave. I have a waiting list of children who would like to come to this school, so if you don't want to comply with what people tell you for your own good, let me know please and I will arrange for your parents to collect you'. This was not directed at me, I was only overhearing, but it made me think that he was right. People had gone without so that I could go to the school of my choosing, and yes, I was grateful enough to try and make the best of the opportunities I was being given. I wasn't good all the time and got into a few scrapes, but deep down I did try because I wanted my whole family to know I was appreciative and thankful. I loved them all so much.

Short skirts, regulation knickers and the school hat

A teacher who was referred to as Head of the Girls announced 'Will all the girls remain in the hall after assembly?'

Wondering what we could have done wrong en masse, we sat there thinking about what was to come. Then she said 'It has come to my attention that some of you girls who have been influenced by recent fashions have started to roll your skirts over at the waist band to make them shorter. So I want all the girls form by form to kneel on the floor and I will be measuring your skirt to ensure that it does not exceed four inches from the ground to the bottom of your skirt'. Some of the girls started to unroll their skirts, with the exception of the year above us, older girls in the fifth form, who through good needleworking skills had managed to cut a foot off and re-hem them. This was a skill we fourth-formers had yet to accomplish. So the fourth form and some of the third girls had their skirts rolled up. The first and second year girls hadn't yet mastered the art of disobedience or in fact succumbed to fashion.

By the time the measuring stick had got to the fourth form we each had nine inches of creased skirt near to the waistband and we were all miraculously wearing the regulation length of skirt. Some of us, despite unrolling the skirt, found that our skirts were still a little on the short side, but we managed to undo the zip and pull the skirt even lower to attain the regulation length. However, one false move and embarrassment could have ensued.

After the usual lecture about giving the school a bad name and the fact we were there to do school work and not attract attention, we were told that legs were to get us from A to B and not for teasing boys or displaying fashions. Those of us who disagreed and cited Twiggy and Mary Quant as our role models lost the customary house point for cheekiness - again!

We walked out of the school hall, and by the time we reached the classroom for the first lesson all skirts were re-rolled to an unsuitable length. This became a regular event, and by the time I had reached the top year fifth-formers had two skirts, one to wear to assembly and then it was a quick dash back to change before lessons began. If she saw us during the day we quickly crouched down to pick something up. Either she thought we were very clumsy or she really couldn't be bothered to pursue the matter. She probably had better things to do with her time than worry about skirt length day in, day out.

For some reason we also supplemented this short skirt craze with a long tie craze, because it gave an illusion of wearing an even shorter skirt. It was not cool to wear a cardigan, jumper or school hat either, so we dispensed with these too as soon as we went into the fourth form.

Regulation thick grey knickers hardly lasted the first year. I swear that had they been worn for five years they would have lasted the course and more, but we hated them. So other styles were introduced, hipsters being the favourite, thinner, tinier and multi-coloured, albeit not allowed. These could not be sent to the laundry each week, but had to be hand-washed and dried where they would not be found. They were pegged under your bed, in the shoe locker, or our favourite place was where the cases were stored. A few adventurous girls hung knickers outside their windows or on dormitory beams, but these were the ones that were usually caught and had them confiscated in the early days, although attitudes changed later as it was generally accepted that it was part of growing up to follow fashion, and there were less restriction on what we were allowed to wear. I remember Matron telling us that the knickers were designed to keep nether regions warm. I remember too the silly look we had on our faces when she said it! We must have just reached that age of not believing everything we had been told, which was in fact probably about twelve and a half!

Most of us though wore long or short socks, even into the last year during school, although tights and bare legs were acceptable at the weekend.

It was a ritual that underwear was placed at the bottom of your bed every evening to wear the next day. In my whole time at Fyfield I never wore a vest. My mother hadn't bought me any because I was allergic, but she had sent a note to Matron on my first day of school to say that I would be wearing my cardigan or blazer so I should not get cold. Matron accepted this, as my mother had been a nurse.

Our parents were pleased that we looked after our jumpers and hats so well that they rarely needed replacing and were nearly always sold on to the next generation of Fyfieldians. We had the idea of re-cycling well before it became fashionable.

One thing we all liked was blazers. They were long, very long, and had lots of pockets to carry around pens, pencils, sweets, hankies, money, paper, bracelets and letters. Generally by the fifth year our blazers were below the length of our skirts too. Prefects had braiding sewn on (the school colours) around the edge of their blazers. I remember my mother saying 'For goodness sake, why did you have to become a prefect? Let's hope your Nan has the time for all this sewing.'

After the first three years we were allowed to change our school shirts from blue to white, which we all did. Sock colour also changed from grey to white. Our Tuf serviceable lace-up shoes were replaced by shoes without laces or straps in the last year and earlier if possible. My favourite shoes were a pair of Mary Janes.

We had a summer dress that was quite a reasonable style and made of nice material, but it also meant you had to keep it clean for a time too, whereas when you wore a shirt you could have a clean one on every day. I can remember that by the fourth year we had seen the last of summer dresses, as only the younger years seemed to wear them.

In my first few years of school, there were metal cages at the back of the hall just as you entered the building. Each person had a section where you kept your indoor shoes and you had to change them every single time you went in or out of the building. Later however this was dispensed with, because the lovely hall floor had a new cover called a canvas drugget floor protection cover, which guarded against damage from chairs, tables and other equipment. Teams of children held the covering and ran from one side of the hall to the other whilst the rest of us stood around to watch. We then put our dining room chairs on top of the floor covering, and returned them to the dining room after assembly.

At weekends we were allowed to wear 'casuals', but girls very rarely wore trousers of any sort. I can only ever remember wearing a very very short dress or very very short skirt and top. When I say short, I mean so short that you couldn't bend over at all and in fact it did wonders for posture, as standing upright had to be maintained at all times.

Fashions played a big part of school life because they were evolving like never before during the 60s. By the time we were 15 we all owned psychedelic dresses which we wore to the school evening dances. Dances were arranged for the two top forms and for everyone on special occasions such as Halloween and Christmas, when the school hall was decorated magnificently.

From 1965 to 1970 skirts just became shorter and shorter, tights had replaced stockings, and slingback shoes became fashionable. Long dresses called 'maxis' were also making an appearance, as some liked to follow the new hippy fashion. The very worst of fashion was a new material that could drip dry called Crimplene, and nearly all girls had one of these dresses. The only advantage they had was that you could wash them and wear them the next day and they never needed ironing.

The boys' trousers were becoming more and more flared, whereas their sports shorts were becoming tighter and tighter. The girls' shorts were tight too, because this was another craze, taking your shorts in at the sides so they were tight. Even a male teacher or two participated in this fashion. Not that we Fifth Form girls ever noticed! But the shorts mutual appreciation society was born. Not only that, but having large breasts and taken-in shorts just made breasts seem even larger, and it did get you attention. Never had so many boys asked me for help with their maths prep! I was just thankful that there was one subject in school that I was good at. You could wear shorts like this, but you couldn't actually do any activity in them.

I remember that there was one girl in the school who was an instant dressmaker. She could run up a dress or adapt clothing almost overnight. She was in the year above me, and every evening when we had a school dance she would turn up in something newly made. She had an eye for fashion too and some of her clothes were very trendy, which caused a bit of talk among everyone. She was very helpful when I wanted to take in the side of my shorts. My shorts had always been a bit baggy and the fashion was to wear them tight. She explained how to do it and when I gave her a blank look, she took them off me, measured me and did it for me. Within the hour they were returned and I spent the next hour practising bending down and over, just to make sure I could and that they didn't spill. I was thrilled with the result, despite not being able to run in them. She was my very first role model.

For games we wore maroon culottes, which enabled us to move around swiftly. They looked like a short skirt and teamed well with an Aertex blouse. We had at some stage a choice of light blue, the traditional colour, or creamy yellow.

As Fyfield was a school for children from the borough of West Ham, the school colours were the same as the West Ham football team, blue and maroon. Hard luck for those of us that supported Spurs or the Orient.

Geometric hair styling was also very popular, with the invention of the bob and the angular shape. Perms were a thing of the past. However I believe most of my year just had a natural style, which meant it grew, and then you had either the fringe or the length trimmed. Boys' hair was catching up in length to ours, which was mainly shoulder length or longer. I can only remember going to Fyfield with a bob, which frankly looked ridiculous, and leaving with hair nearly to my waist. Long hair provided me with a mean, menacing look which I liked. At weekends I used to wear rags or sponge rollers to get curls for Saturday. It was worth losing a night's sleep.

The Head of Girls, Polly, constantly reminded the girls with long hair that their ears were not taxi doors, in other words we were not to put hair behind them but wear a hair band. This is why girls in most of the 1960s photographs wore headbands. Some girls just kept their hair short to save the bother. It seemed so unfair when the boys' hair was allowed to hang loose, but there wasn't any equality in those days. We were allowed to plait hair or have a pony tail or even a more sophisticated hairstyle, as long as it looked tidy. Until the change of headmaster boys had to have a hair inspection and be ordered to get it cut, but the next headmaster didn't seem to worry about things like that and from what I remember he had fairly untamed hair himself.

Every year when ex-pupils returned for Speech Day presentations, note was taken of what they were wearing after leaving school. This set our fashion trend. In the year I returned I wore a mid-brown suit and cream blouse that my Nan advised as being smart, but a lot of my year wore maxi dresses and hippy-style clothes. I was already at work and never really had the opportunity to experiment with colour or fun clothes, as the Civil Service code of dress was sombre colours, brown or navy blue with a white or cream blouse and stockings with appropriate slip-on court shoes, no sling backs, and mackintoshes were to be black, navy or grey. Mine was grey. It never bothered me that much, as it was really just swapping one uniform for another. The only real difference was that I wore make-up every day. The Civil Service changed quickly in the Seventies and became far more relaxed. When I returned in 1973 after trying one or two other jobs, you could wear whatever fashion you wanted. I wore very short miniskirts. I kept my hair very long too and my heels got higher by about an inch a year. It remained that way until I reached the sensible age of twenty eight.

Sick Bay

Sick Bay was a building with two wards, one for boys and another for girls, a small isolation room with just three beds, a treatment room, a store cupboard and a kitchen, together with Matron's own quarters.

I quickly volunteered to become a Sick Bay monitor. This involved doing chores for Matron whenever she asked for help. There was a whole small team of girls who helped.

We usually helped in pairs and most of the chores were to do with serving meals and running errands for those who were sick. We also stocked Matron's treatment room with supplies under her strict supervision.

I remained a Sick Bay helper for the whole five years at school. Matron knew my mother was a nurse and my dad a laboratory technician, so it was likely that I had an interest in health. One of the features that enticed me to become a helper was that the helpers had to make fresh toast for those who were sick, every day. This task was always done just as Matron took herself off to the staff room for breakfast. It provided us with a small window of opportunity to make delicious hot buttered toast for those in the bay and then for ourselves. We did however carefully count out how many slices of bread that would be per patient and hope that someone had a sore throat and was too ill to eat the toast. We always thought Matron had never rumbled us, but on the last day of my time in the school, when I was saying my goodbyes, she told me she had known all along.

Some of the girls liked to volunteer so that they could visit the boys' room in Sick Bay, but personally I found that there was nothing attractive in seeing boys in their pyjamas, especially sick boys. I always chose the girls side to help in.

Another of the aspects that encouraged us girls to become monitors was information and reading material. Matron's shelf was full of books which were full of useful information, and many of us used to diagnose our own ailments without the need to see her, and even treat ourselves if the opportunity arose. I will never forget the day

Matron returned unexpectedly to find me carving away at my foot with a scalpel, trying to remove a verruca. Matron never left the treatment room door open again; it was always firmly locked when she went to breakfast. She told me off very sternly. I had a good talking to about trust and how she had thought me, up until then, a sensible girl.

The local doctor came to school twice a week to a verruca clinic, and Matron explained to him what I'd been up to, in the hope that I would feel so embarrassed I wouldn't do it again, but he just found the whole scenario quite amusing. Over the years we got on splendidly, as I found he was a good resource when I was the only person in the last two years of school to study biology and human biology. He asked me what I most enjoyed about the subjects and I remember telling him dissection and labelling the dissection, and he replied 'Now why doesn't that surprise me?' There couldn't have been many pupils that could enthuse so much about a pig's heart, a kidney or a bull's eye.

There were two occasions when Sick Bay was so full that dormitories had to be isolated and used for pupils, and this happened twice to my knowledge in my time there. The biggest of these was a very serious influenza epidemic in the winter of 1966. Practically everyone succumbed to the virus, teaching staff, the headmaster and eighty per cent of the pupils. The Friends of Fyfield School Association arranged for some of the parents to come to the school to assist by nursing, cleaning and serving meals. I remember that the mothers set up their make-do camp beds in what was then the Common Room, but I don't think they actually got very much sleep or rest.

I was helping Matron for long periods in Sick Bay, and I too caught it. I was very seriously ill at one point and eventually I was sent home by the doctor for a month to try and recuperate after the illness. After I had become dangerously ill I remember the doctor came to see me three times in one day, and the following day I felt a lot better. I was, at this stage, in the isolation room with two other girls, who with me were the worst affected by the virus. I hated having to be at home and was itching to get back to school. Fortunately the outcome was good for everyone. However my Great Gran died during that bad UK flu epidemic.

When you were in Sick Bay you could look out toward the orchard and watch the birds or gaze across fields. The crows often used to wake you first thing, before even Matron was up on a cold and frosty morning. Occasionally you could also hear arguments from the staff houses, usually one of the teachers telling their own children to hurry up. On a Sunday you could just hear church bells in the distance. My favourite sound was the calling of the crows.

Matron used to give us magazines to read in bed when we were sick and this helped us to grow up. Our favourite page was the problem page. Quite frankly I couldn't really understand why people would want to ask someone they didn't know a very personal question, but of course once you had read the question, the answers were most enlightening. This definitely supplemented our sex education. If the article was exceptionally good we used to rip it out of the magazine and circulate it among our year group. As a separate pastime we read the question out loud and in turn made up our own solutions to problems, much to the amusement of Matron, who pretended that she hadn't heard most of the time, but when she couldn't help but hear she used to say, 'How very interesting, my bevy of beauties, I must remember that in case anyone needs advice'. At this point we all fell about laughing, and she then deemed us well enough to be discharged from Sick Bay and back to school. Matron had a lovely soft side to her personality and you could talk to her about anything if you got on well with her. One of my friends said she was like Marmite. Apparently Matron had disliked her from the word go.

The beds in Sick Bay were far superior to your dormitory bed and making them was a monitor's job, overseen by Matron. They were a delight to sleep in, but I always managed to make a miraculous recovery, like most, before a period of double Art.

It was also a place where you could go to escape assembly in the early years. At the time when chairs were introduced assembly became a battlefield. I had scars both on the back and front of my legs, mainly from chairs put there by boys who used them as weapons.

One of my worst accidents at school was when I tripped coming out of the New School block and fell knees first onto a boot-scraper made of metal. Not only did my books go flying, at the point of impact the metal cut deeply into my skin and I couldn't move. Friends rushed to help me up but the pain was so bad. Blood was gushing out of my knees and although they were pulling to get me up, I felt very faint. Matron came rushing from Sick Bay to help. I had two very swollen knees and the scabs, in long, deep lines, lasted for a long time. I was banned from going swimming for weeks, and I still have the scars.

Matron used to have her mother to stay. I remember she seemed very old to us at the time, though she probably wasn't. One day Matron said her mother would appreciate it if we went to have a chat. At the time she was crocheting a mat. I thought that was clever, so she then taught me to crochet and I made a small white mat for my bedside cabinet. I still have it.

Sick Bay was always busy, with verruca treatment the number one activity, but there was always measuring, weighing pupils and a variety of other ailments to deal with as well as the usual childhood illness of mumps, measles and chicken pox. There were also quite a few sports injuries. Matron also had her role as a support during times of bad news, so she matron had her work cut out.

Sick bay wasn't just about being ill; it was a good resource centre too.

Open Days

Open Days were when your family came to school to see what you and everyone else had been doing in lessons and generally examine your work. The proud relatives needed an opportunity to compare you favourably to other children.

You were expected to meet your family and walk around

the school with them between 2 pm and 4 pm. They were allowed to visit places that were normally off limits to parents, so there was a grand tour of your classrooms, the art room, library, needlework room, domestic science room, metalwork room, library, common rooms and many other places, but neither you nor they were allowed into the dormitories or the dining room.

Everyone went to your classroom and was allowed to look at your work books, including your rough book. My rough book was, like many others, filled with pop stars' names, hearts and arrows and some very silly doodles (yes those silly doodles!) as was pointed out to me. My Dad even said that he could take it home to re-cover it, in brown paper, such was his embarrassment.

On one occasion in English Studies we had read a play and were all recorded on tape, which in 1966 was quite unusual. I managed to get my parents to listen to it, although they were not all that keen. I was expecting them to say how well I'd done, but instead my Mum, being a nurse, typically said she thought I had sinus trouble and my Dad just went on and on about how the tape recorder worked. They were both totally oblivious to anything I actually said. Nor were they into stories. To be worthwhile, books for my Dad had to be non-fiction and preferably about motorbikes or aeroplanes. My mother liked stories but only romance or crime, neither of which I had a clue about. So my stories on safe subjects like 'What I did in my holidays', 'My favourite pet' etc scored somewhere between zero and one in readability and interest. Not only that but neither of them were really into adjectives either.

I can only remember my Dad looking through my maths workbook and saying that he was very pleased that I could do that level of maths, as some of his students at technical college couldn't do what I was doing. My Mum wouldn't have commented as she didn't do maths. Life was far simpler for her. Wood was a bit or a big bit, recipes (which rarely worked) were items thrown into a mixing bowl, and put into the oven, and it was the oven's fault if they were a disaster. It was also the reason she wasn't strict on time. She could not deduct one figure from another on the clock, so she hadn't the foggiest whether we were early or late home. Hence meals arrived when they did.

I took them both to see the apron I was making in needlework, but I knew it couldn't have been that good when my Mum asked what it was. Then when I told her she said it would be OK when it was finished, and I said it was finished.

Our trip to the art room wasn't much better. They both enthused about some boys' drawings and how good he was and then asked where was mine and said 'what is it?' When I said 'abstract', they said 'oh it's nice and blue, but what is it meant to be?' They didn't quite comprehend the idea of 'abstract'. I said in desperation that it was a piece of linoleum. I could tell they were not impressed. Then they looked at the pottery and I pointed out mine and they were both quite liked my little dish - result!

It was the same every year. They were never really into school work. For my mother it was about the enjoyment school could give, by being outdoors, nice air in the countryside, having friends and wearing a nice uniform. Dad was a little bit different as subjects that he liked interested him, so Art, Cooking, English, History, Geography, Religious Education, Music (except opera) and Sport were not on his list. Only Mathematics and Rural Science were on his list, so constructive conversation and praise was a bit restricted, really.

I just loved the way my parents looked at other children's work and were unimpressed by their achievements if they didn't like the parents and went overboard with praise if they did. They divided other parents into categories of like and dislike. Anyone who was in charge, loud, bold or boasting of their offspring's achievements was on the dislike list. Anyone who was quiet, sweet, meek and utterly charming was on the like list, unless they were only pretending. I often wondered whether all parents were like this.

Funnily enough, by the time my brother joined the school and they had to trawl around two lots of work on display, they had lost interest in mine completely. At this time my parents started inviting my grandparents to come to the school, and I liked this very much as no matter how awful my work was, they thought it beautiful and like no other. They were so very encouraging, despite not understanding the content, and always wanted a copy of it. If it was a load of rubbish, they said I had lovely handwriting. If it was Art they said it was good use of colour. Never a bad word was said about my efforts, or my brother's.

That's the benefit of grandparents. Not only that, but they returned to tell aunties and uncles about how very clever you were, and before long the whole extended family were praising your efforts.

After the parents had left we had supper and school got back to normal, but there was no letter-writing home that weekend. I loved those family days. For me the education had been my parents' reaction, and swapping stories with other girls about what their parents had said about my work and theirs.

Chapter Seven

EVERYTHING YOU EVER WANTED TO KNOW ABOUT THE DRYING ROOM AND MORE

The Drying Room was in the quadrangle, strategically placed next to the Fifth Form girls' Senior Common Room. In the Senior Common Room during the last year of school, girls had lockers to keep their belongings in instead of desks. This was convenient, because the room was very central to everywhere and it enabled you to get to the library, school block, dining room and phone easily. It also had a few comfy chairs and a television. We all loved our Senior Common Room. It had been decorated and furnished by a couple of the Third Form girls as a project during 1969. It was the place to hang out and chat. Unless, of course you had a boyfriend, and then it was just a convenient stop-off to dump your books and pencil case before going to the Drying Room next door.

The Drying Room was a big warm room used mainly to dry swimwear and a few undies that girls had washed themselves. We had a good school laundry service, but we could get our swimwear dry in a matter of hours and re-use it again the same day if we wanted. That was the idea of the room. It had large wooden frames that were angled from front to back in a zigzag. It had great big white extractor fans built into the structure that were really noisy. Obviously swimwear involved a swim towel too, so they were also placed on the racks. Some days the room was so full of drying clothes that it was hot and steamy and difficult to see precisely who was there. In the early years we used to respect the rule that girls' and boys' areas of the drying room were separate, but by the time you got to the last year you knew the excuses – there wasn't any room, you saw someone's items had accidentally fallen from the rack and were just replacing them, garments needed turning round to get dry. The most pathetic excuse was 'I got my left muddled up with my right, so I accidentally went to the wrong area'.

It was not surprising that during that last year a lot of the Fifth Form boys used to use the quadrangle as a short cut and suddenly disappear before reaching the far end of it. They had a lot of washing to dry too.

As lots of the fifth-formers were sixteen or so, it was inevitable that there would be lots of 'couples', and the Drying Room was a favourite place for them. I was a lookout for a couple of my best friends. If a teacher or Matron was spotted I would give a bang on the wall, but in time we had to develop more sophisticated signalling as people became wise to it. With one couple, the girl would be in the room with some washing over her arm and if signalled the boy would jump onto the rack so that whoever was looking couldn't see their feet, although occasionally if they fell off the teacher would become wise to it and go to examine the spot and venture into the room. The windows were fixed, so there really was only one way out and that was via the door. The best-ever disguise was when a boy wrapped himself in a towel and balanced on the top rack trying not to be noticed.

If a teacher spotted you, it was usually punishment for the boy, although to be fair some of the teachers didn't actually do anything other than tell them both to go. Matron however was a different kettle of fish. One look from Matron was enough to make you shiver. Matron had no upper level of embarrassment; she would talk to you about it leading on to something else and what the consequences of that were. She used to say that she had radar and she would be keeping a close eye on the situation and if she ever got really cross, she shouted at you. Nobody wanted to cross Matron.

The other side was that of the boy and girl. Firstly boys don't care, you can shout, punish, humiliate and try to bargain, but once they have their sights set on a girl and are in a relationship, the girl is all they care about. So this was a losing battle. Whatever was said to them they ignored and just carried on regardless. They even expected their punishment, and I remember one boy digging over the rural science plot twice before he had even been caught, just to get ahead of the game. Girls were slightly different in as much as they tried to carry on regardless but be more discreet and not get caught. They were better at planning, and more cunning. They used to weigh up that teachers were keen to eat, and knew when they were likely to be busy. Two key times to meet would be meal times if you could get away with it, or a trip to Sick Bay when assembly was on, only neither of the couple had time to actually go to the sick bay and if caught out at all, they were banned from going out in assembly time. Another was picking up the post if they could meet en route. If the Guinness Book of Records ever needed a 'snogging' record, the Fyfield Drying Room would probably hold the record, either that or for the amount of washing dried in any one day or possibly both in tandem.

Then one day something terrible happened. The Headmaster said that the drying room was going to be cleared every day of items and emptied completely. Shock and horror prevailed, and as Matron once said, 'Don't even think of meeting in the Orchard unless you can make yourself look like a tree'.

As for more, I let my best friend have the library store cupboard key until one teacher realised what was going on by peeping through the keyhole after being alerted to unusual sounds that did not sound like sorting out books.

There was also an area under the stage where couples went, as in my last year a couple was caught there and there was a real fuss made about it. I think someone may have even been expelled because of it.

However, one avenue that was undiscovered was about a two-mile bike ride away adjacent to a public footpath. The idea was that the boy signed out with friend, both with bikes, to Fyfield village and the girls signed out to Ongar in a group and then a boy and girl met up, to rejoin their original parties for the return to school. It was common for girls to sit on the saddle and the boys to just stand to pedal the bike to enable them to get to Spains Wood, Willingale.

I didn't have a boyfriend. They were all fairly nice chaps, but I was almost a year younger than some of the other girls and having a boyfriend just didn't appeal to me. I did get a lift on the bike to the woods, but the boy wanted some help with his maths prep and didn't want to been seen asking me in school. This suited me.

The last day of school

It wasn't the last time I ever visited Fyfield, but I clearly remember my last day of school.

As usual with all school leavers, the last few weeks, especially after exams have finished, are exciting. There is lots of reminiscing and swapping stories about what you are going to do in the future. Some people's plans were tinged with sadness. One girl's parents had decided that the family were going to emigrate to Australia, and for her it was just terrible. I remember her crying most of the time and I felt awful for her, knowing that she was going to be so far away from us, even though Australia did sound a nice place. Not that I really knew where it was. I'd seen it on a globe, but at fifteen years old I had no sense of distance. All she told us was that the ship would take weeks to get there, so I knew that it must be far, far away.

We signed each other's autograph books, swapped addresses and promised to keep in touch with one another. We took our last walk around the field, savouring every step.

I sold most of my uniform and my hockey stick to other girls, along with everything else I didn't need any more, including the trunk I had used for five years. I packed what was left into a bag. My life's possessions were in one small bag. We said our goodbyes to everyone. It was the end of term for all, but the end of an era for the leavers. We had seen previous years' leavers return and tell us what work they had, and that made the new world we were facing seem quite inviting. Some girls already had some work lined up and knew what they were going to be doing.

I wasn't going home; I went to stay with a very good friend and her sister for a week. I was putting off going home to the dreary new place the family had moved to. The place that had robbed me of the familiarity I felt comfortable with, the place where getting about was easy. I loved London and just despised Benfleet, which was the suburbia of Southend-on-Sea. If anyone has ever been to Tarpots Corner, they will understand exactly what I mean. It has one main road that is fume-filled, busy and traffic laden without any redeeming features. Traffic thunders along the road to London during the morning and returns during the evening. Tarpots Corner had a rundown pub with tarpots standing outside it, a petrol station that dominated one side of the road and a small row of 1960s shops, including Liptons, a very small supermarket (which really made me wonder how it could be referred to as 'super', let alone a 'market'), a hardware shop, hairdressers, two banks and a coffee shop. My parents told me it would give me a better life, and like many others who moved from London, it was considered a step up. I hadn't quite figured out how in my own mind and when I questioned them, they said it just would and it was for my benefit, without any explanation.

Some of the girls were in a similar boat, returning to places their parents had moved to, places they didn't really know.

The day arrived and it was the most gloriously sunny beautiful day. It was 17th July. The day started in the usual way with us going to the last breakfast. Already the nervousness and sadness had begun to build inside me. Returning to dormitory after breakfast seemed strange. Usually there was excitement about what we were going to do in the holidays, but all there was now was lots of luggage and the messy pieces you get when you are moving. All the beds were stripped, pink candlewick counterpanes neatly folded on top of blankets and pillows and large sacks of sheets ready for the laundry. Everything had started to look bare and used. There was a last-minute giveaway of things we really didn't need, a last minute double check of everyone's addresses and then transferring belongings after the very last look of the dormitory, Queens 1, to the school dining room, waiting at our tables waiting for the next car to turn up and then shout goodbye to that person, until it was your turn.

Our names were called, mine and my friend's and her sister. Her Dad had arrived and somehow the tension had built up inside me. I started to cry. It was more of a howl than a cry and it drew a lot of attention. My friend's Dad said he could take me home if I preferred to do that, and could quite understand that I was unhappy. The Headmaster said that if I couldn't face leaving I could stay another year, as I was only fifteen and he could contact my parents if that was what I would like. My friend was very upset too, but because I was crying, not because she was leaving. It was eventually agreed that I would go as planned to stay with my friend and her Dad told us that we should have fun before we started work. He started to tell us of all the things we could do in the next couple of weeks and I cheered up. Her sister was quite peeved that we had held up 'going home', as she had another couple of years to go at school.

My friend's Dad suggested that we start the leaving process off with a party for the disposal of our 'grey battleships' (battleship-grey knickers) as soon as we got home and have cake, ice cream etc and bin that underwear. He reliably told us that was what Agas were for. Unknown to anyone, except us of course, we had already left our clean, neatly folded grey battleships in places throughout school, to be found by the returners. I left mine placed in saucepans in the Domestic Science room. Everyone had positioned them in not so obvious places, so they would just keep turning up for months!

We went to Surrey for the week and had a lovely time, visiting the Epsom racecourse, London shopping, Hampton Court and trying to visit a theatre in Guildford, but not quite getting to grips with train timetables. At Hampton Court I lost my hat in the Thames as it was windy, got lost in the maze and generally had a good time. On the theatre trip we both gave up trying to find Guildford and eventually found a phone box at Effingham Junction to call my friend's Dad to come and pick us up. However neither of us wanted to say Effingham because it sounded rude, so we described where we were and made him guess. He arrived and kept teasing us both about the name and mentioning it all week, until it became a joke. In those days young ladies did not swear, and they went red when someone else did.

The following week my friend came to stay with me. We spent most of our time well outside Benfleet, visiting Pitsea Market, my Nan, Leigh Old Town and Southend pier. At the end of the pier we went into a booth to record us both singing and talking on vinyl. We had lunch in the Wimpey Bar and we both felt very grown up.

The following week I started work in Southend and evening classes in Leigh on Sea. I would be with adults, have an income and go out for lunch every day. There was also a lot of office banter and some odd rituals, like having your own hand towel and having to queue to get a clean one each week, and having to sit at your desk with your feet up whilst the floor was mopped by a cleaner once a week.

The downside of work was that I was the youngest by at least twenty years. On the positive side, I could wear what

I want, have my hair how I wanted, use perfume, wear jewellery and take the dog out when I wanted, and the cat could sleep on my bed. I had my own radio to listen to the pirate stations, and a second hand record player. My brother was still at school, so I had a lot of peace and quiet too. So not everything was bad.

I would be learning new skills at evening classes, where I had signed on for a year's course in shorthand and typing. Both classes were small, but I enjoyed the familiarity of the classroom setting. I was surprised that there were more men learning shorthand and typing than women, and that after an hour we stopped for a tea break. I completed the course in both and the following year ventured into Art and Badminton classes. At 16 I was never too tired to go out every night and enjoy myself after a day's work.

The weekends were a round of visiting family, shopping and going out. I never watched television as I wasn't in the habit. I spent a lot of time planning where I was going to travel to and started off by investigating the local area on my own. So by the time I returned to Fyfield at the beginning of October, to the school prize giving, I was well into the world of work and the yearning for school life had subsided.

Important visitors

A tall Scottish man who wore a bow tie called Fyfe Robertson came to Fyfield to make a documentary for the BBC. It was featured in a programme called 'Twenty-Four

Hours' which was a long-running daily news magazine programme shown some time after 10pm. It featured in-depth but short documentary films that determined the method and approach of current affairs programmes. It was quite exciting, as I saw him come out of the staff dining room and make his way over to the teaching block with one of the teachers. At that time I sat with my back to the door that exited the dining room on the far side so I managed to get a good view of all comings and goings, both to and from the Staff Room. I had seen him on television and thought he was quite old at that time.

Some time during 1966 Dr Royston Lambert came to Fyfield to carry out a study which was later included in his book called 'The Hothouse Society'. He stayed at Fyfield for about two weeks and I remember that he talked to quite a lot of the pupils. I have read the book and thought that the content which was supplied by pupils of different boarding schools was interesting. It does give you an insight into life at boarding school, but no more than that. I suppose it might be the old-fashioned equivalent of our modern day 'reality television'. The imbalance of the material and the way it was arranged throughout the book would, however, probably confirm people's long held prejudices about Boarding School, most of which still exists today despite various governments' attempts to convince society that opportunities are equal and children's needs are all different.

On another occasion a film producer called Julian Ashton made a film about growing old and the attitude of young people towards old people. I was filmed for this and when it was shown on television at 11.20 pm, we were woken and were allowed to get out and go to the Common Room to watch it. There were only snippets from about four pupils and I was one of them, talking about how when I got older I would try to do things to keep myself young and keep my appearance looking young, because that way you would stay young and have young attitudes and probably a better understanding of the young. Although it is fair to say, I did break my arm at a roller disco when I was in my forties, bought myself a sports car in my fifties and am technologically up there with the rest! As far as my appearance goes I think that like many others I am ageing gracefully - or not, but I still don't fit the elderly stereotype or conform that well either. To actually be on television and be speaking for a long time was such a big thing in the 60s, but to be honest I forgot about it very quickly. My family didn't, and I was embarrassed about it for ages.

The series it appeared as part of was called 'Scene', which tackled a huge range of social issues and was primarily made for school television, but some of the episodes were shown on late-night television for adults. Some time later in 1970 Julian Ashton came to the school and brought the film with him for the Additional English Studies pupils to watch. Younger pupils thought it was interesting to see some of their fellow pupils in the film.

Dormitories and boot lockers

I can remember the boys' dormitories were named Merton,

Trinity, Churchill and Kings and the girls were Clare, Sommerville, Newham/Derwent and Queens. All the dormitories were completely different in size and nature.

Clare One to Four were small dormitory rooms, taking about eight beds each with prefects' rooms in the middle. It was situated on one side of the quadrangle, which looked onto a field one side and into the quadrangle the other.

Somerville was adjacent to Clare, but ran the whole length with little separation at all, apart from a couple of cubicles in the middle. You really couldn't see out of any of the windows, despite there being many of them. It was also very draughty when the far end door was opened and the wind blew in from the sheltered section of the quadrangle. It was a wind tunnel. I think I felt cold all the time I was in Somerville. I neither liked the dormitory nor the open feeling. I hated the lack of privacy. I only spent one term there.

Newham was a new 1960s block that had only just been built. It had vinyl floors instead of wood and big windows, all around. It was spacious and airy, but on the downside, if you visited the dormitory during the day (which was not allowed), you were very likely to get caught. There were four dormitories to this block, one on each corner. I was in the one that was most visible to passers-by, and it probably accounts for why I lost more house points that year.

Queens was much smaller, with only two rooms, Queens One and Two. It was also very slightly sunken down, so when you looked out of the windows you felt lower down. This was probably because it was built adjacent to a slope.

The Clare dormitories were by far my favourite ones as

you felt in the true hub of things, whereas Queens was by far the quietest, being on the edge, although to be fair you knew just as much about what was happening as you could see everyone coming and going. In the girl's dormitories, all the counterpanes and curtains were pink.

I can't say I know very much about the boys' dormitories, as I can only recall visiting them four times. Once was when I was initially shown around the school, another when my brother's housemaster asked to see me, a further time when we went to Churchill to watch the landing on the moon on television and again when I did a stint of babysitting for one of the staff, who was housed adjacent to the boys' dormitory.

When you returned to start a new term, the dormitories had their own smell. They had been spring-cleaned very thoroughly and smelt new and very clean. You could smell the polish that had been used on the floors before you even opened the door. It was always best to get back as early as you could, so that you could bagsy the best bed and space or next to whom you wanted to, or in fact and more importantly away from those that irritated you. There was nothing worse than being next to some dullard or someone who was always in trouble, as if things went wrong for them you were constantly being asked what had happened and there was nothing worse than splitting. My policy was to stay well away from anyone who was dull or trouble.

I progressed during my five years through all of them, starting in Clare One, progressing the second year to Somerville, it being the posh end of Sommerville, for one term, then to Clare Four next, followed by back to Clare One and then into Newham Three and lastly Queens One. I had a stint in my own room in Queens and again in Sommerville, where I had a cubicle that was situated right in the middle of the dormitory and separated the part that was now used by the first year girls and that used by the second. However my very last term was in Queens One, which I was quite happy about as we had more prefects, so we had to take turns at having a room. Not only that but it was right opposite the library, which was convenient, and I did have someone to talk to after lights out. On one occasion one of the prefects that had the single room in the same block came through and told us off for talking after lights out and then arranged for us to lose a house point. I felt very aggrieved that one of my fellow prefects had taken a house point off me in the last year and me a prefect, so that marked the end of our otherwise good relationship for good. I never spent any time with her again and nor did anyone else in our dormitory.

Clare One had the disadvantage of being adjacent to the teacher's room, but it had the advantage of housing one of the very nicest teachers, during my first year. Only occasionally did she tell us off for talking after lights out and then only when it had just gone on too long. I remember to this day the very light clip of her kitten heels as she came to her room, some time after we had all gone to bed.

Then I went into the worst end of Sommerville, so that when you wanted to visit the bathroom, you had to go outside under the covered part of the Quad, and across to it.

It had a row of showers without any curtains, as I remember, and a big boot room. There were two choices, shower and get dried in the freezing cold and go back to the dormitory or keep your towel wrapped around, put on your dressing gown and slippers and go back to the dormitory to dry, by which time, when you had got there, you were probably dry anyway. Also you hoped that you had showered so early that no one was using the pay phone, which was in a little open-air covered way just prior to our shower room. At seven thirty it was a mad dash to the shower room at full speed. There wasn't any privacy whatever you choose, but it didn't really seem to bother us that much. You just got used to it.

By the second year I was only in the posh end of Somerville with twelve girls for one term, I don't know why, but I was moved the following term to Clare Four. I had been with the noisy crowd for the term and then was part of the quietest group of girls ever. None of us really liked this arrangement because it sort of divided our year. Although we were joined by a corridor and used the same washing facilities and boot room, I always had the feeling that I was missing out on some fun. Clare Four though was by far superior accommodation to Sommerville. For one thing it was small, so it was very much warmer. It had the added advantage that everyone walked through it, day and night, so you saw everyone. It also had the attraction of looking out directly onto the field, and anyone on their way to the swimming pool could be seen. You could even hear the splashing of the pool water on summer evenings when our windows were open and also the early-morning swimmers. Then I was moved back to Clare One when there was a change around.

By the fourth year I was in a lovely little dormitory which was part of the new block. It was in the best possible position and I was with a good crowd. It was very handy adjacent to Sick Bay for my duties there. Our boot room and washing facilities were next to the dormitory, so there was less walking and lovely showers, and a bath cubicle which gave more privacy.

The boot room had rows of small lockers, and pegs for coats and outdoor wear. Inside the locker you kept all your shoes and anything that was for the outdoors such as hockey boots and running spikes with their respective cleaning materials. You had to have a lot of cleaning materials. There was a knife for getting off mud, a tin of black shoe polish for school shoes, a liquid white mixture to make plimsolls white, a tin of dubbin to put on sports shoes, spare spikes and a nut to undo and replace worn spikes, wellington boots, casual shoes and slippers. If you misbehaved you could sometimes be punished by having to clean all your shoes and if you'd been very bad, everyone else's too. Shoes for the following day had to be cleaned last thing of an evening and put on the top of your locker for inspection by a prefect. When I became a prefect I rarely gave anyone punishment for poorly-cleaned shoes, but just mentioned it to them to clean them better the following evening. That was unless they irritated me in some other way, which very few did. It probably accounts for why now I go and buy a new pair of shoes when mine get dirty, as I have an aversion to shoe polish.

A boot locker was the place where you had to keep tuck if you had any.

I remember once that someone played a practical joke on me by blowing up a plastic swimming ring and shoving it in my locker, and when I opened the door it gave me a fright as it sprung to life. I knew who had done it and in response I got the groundsman to give me a very big plastic bag full of newly-cut grass, to repay the joke. I stuffed that locker so full of grass that it looked like wedding confetti when she opened it. How we laughed, but I did help her to clear it up. It took hours to get rid of every scrap, but we laughed until we hurt.

Being in Queens was the nearest we had been to a boys' dormitory, and we used to spar with one another as there was only a library that separated us. We were only caught once using a towel with a wet end in a flicking competition. The idea was to wet the end of your towel, take it outside, creep past the library and wait until you saw a boy sneaking over to your dormitory and flick your towel before he did, or if a boy left the library he was fair game too. However the boys did sneak out and into our boot room to play about with our shoes as a dare, and they would come in and swap the lockers around. This used to cause big panic, as the first time you put on your shoes was to breakfast and imagine going to your locker and finding that your items were arranged somewhere else. As the dormitory had two entrances and exit, the boys often use to sneak across to see their girlfriends, but if caught it was very likely they would get expelled, despite us trying to hide them or ignoring them.

Likewise some of the girls used to go across to the boys' dormitories too. I wasn't one of them.

Social time, clubs and activities

One thing I will never forget about Fyfield was that there was never any time or reason to get bored. It just wasn't possible. For just 240 pupils there was a really extraordinary range of activities to choose from in the way of sports, clubs, outings and so on.

From the very moment I got out of bed there was a routine, until I got into bed again at the end of the day. Every member of the teaching staff seemed very enthusiastic about their respective activities, whether it was sport, music, drama, art or an unusual activity. The Deputy Head, who we referred to as 'Polly', although that was not her name to my knowledge, kept us occupied one way or another. She had energy, passion and exuberance about her all the time. Not only that but she moved at the speed of light. Goodness knows how many pairs of shoes she got through. She rarely wore any stockings and she turned her feet outwards, so her shoes looked very worn and used to clip loudly as she walked, so you at least knew when she was approaching.

When I first went to school I didn't really know what I wanted to do in the way of clubs and just signed out to go for a walk most afternoons, but before long I was encouraged to have a go at most things. Some turned out disastrously, such as my attempt at cross-country running. I got lost within the first mile and some hours after everyone else had returned to school I was running around in circles, when I came across my brother, who had also been left behind or taken a wrong turning, so we ran together and got to a signpost saying 'Willingale'. That was when I realised we had run about 3 miles in the wrong direction, so we turned round and headed the other way, only to find a car approaching us. The car stopped and a teacher got out and came towards us asking 'Have you decided to run away from school?' I answered 'er no, quite the opposite, the school seems to have run away from us', or that is what it had felt like. I must have run about 10 miles that day and was totally exhausted. Considering the cross country started at 14.30 and it was now 18.15, I was a bit fed up. From that moment on I wasn't trusted to take part in cross country, thank goodness, as anything that required a sense of direction was not my strongest point. I became a course marshal, just standing there and directing, but even that was a bit hazardous as I sent everyone who had upset me in the wrong direction. It only took two weeks before I was rumbled and assigned to extra Sick Bay duty.

Other activities turned out very well, such as badminton and tennis, because by the time I left school I had joined local clubs and developed my skills further. Other clubs and pastimes such as Guides and Additional English Club, swimming, athletics and table tennis provided a range of enjoyable activity and things to do with friends.

When I was at Fyfield we had Stamp Club, Judo, Guides and Scouts, Junior Social Club, Art, Drama, Car Club, Sailing and Seamanship, Wildlife Club, Additional English Club, Swimming, Hockey, Netball, Cross Country running, Football Cricket, Volley Ball, Athletics, Personal attainment Swimming Club, Rounders, Tennis, Table tennis, Hockey, Softball, Badminton, Orchestra and Choir. We even had a bit of a go at ballet, but most of us were considered too big to participate! We did though participate in country dancing and were given lessons in other dancing, such as the waltz.

On a few occasions I played hockey in the school team, which I enjoyed as we played all weathers. A bit of wind or rain never stopped a match - we just got a bit muddier. I also played netball in the school team. I was better at this because on the plus side I had a good eye for the goal net, although on the minus side I wasn't very tall, so if I got to score before the defender was in front of me, it turned out well.

I joined Art Club because the teacher was lovely. I had no imagination or artistic talent at that age at all. It was just good fun in a place that felt good to be in because of the smell of paint and all the art around the room. Later in life I did go on to paint in oils and take photographs and found the lessons I had learnt about composition and colour were invaluable. Apart from that the Art teacher was always very laid back and never really told anyone off. Even when he went out of class and told us to get on quietly, he always made a noise, so you knew he was returning, and everyone was quiet before he got back into class. He sat there and read his car magazine and we did what we wanted.

I joined the Guides because I liked the uniform, especially the lanyard, hat, and penknife. I enjoyed it because like so many I relished the opportunity to gain badges. My first attempt at gaining a badge was in First Aid. I delighted in bandaging my friends so much that they eventually looked like mummies. I remember one of my friends saying,' I've got two broken arms, two broken legs and ribs, can you stop now as I am getting hot'? We both fell about laughing when I told her it would be so good if she could just faint to add some authenticity to the event, as I'd covered fainting and the recovery position the previous week. Somehow I don't think I ever did acquire my First Aid badge. I never got a Needlework badge or an Orienteering badge or the Athletes' badge either. Not to mention the lack of a Cook's badge! So it was surprising that I even lasted the course.

I did enjoy our Thinking Day and a trip with Patrol leaders to Blake Hall during the Diamond Jubilee Year of 1970. We were told that later in 1970 there would be a road safety competition, so it was good that I left in the July before it took place, otherwise who knows what might have happened.

Some of our social time was spent around and about in the countryside, just lying in a field with a few friends chatting away, mostly about fashion, boys or pop music, our three main informed topics of conversation. In fact my fondest memories of Fyfield are lovely summer afternoons sitting with friends on the school field after having been for a swim, just chatting. I remember that a couple of my friends had a good sense of humour, so we used to unpick and re-wrap every personality in the school.

Chapter Eight

THE BENEFITS OF BOARDING SCHOOL

People tend to fall into one of two categories when you speak to them about boarding schools - they tend to hate them or love them. The only thing that seems a bit odd to me is that quite a few people hate them without any real reason. It is like life really, if you have an open mind you can learn first and decide after, but if you close your mind before you even have the facts or any experience, you miss out on some wonderful things.

A lot of people are persuaded by the media, which sensationalise small negative stories about boarding school and the pupils that go to them, and that is what catches people's interest.

People sometimes have very negative views about boarding, which they use to rationalise their own behaviour.

I learnt this very early on when various people I met said something like 'oh you poor thing, being sent away to school'. They had made a few assumptions, like the fact that I had no choice in the matter, whereas I had lots of choice, and that my parents had done something bad, whereas in fact, they had made sacrifices for my benefit, or home life was very difficult, but in fact it was fairly comfortable and middle class. It was also very loving and very family-orientated. Sometimes people put it on a par with being sent to Borstal or prison and made comments about being locked up at school. Surprisingly enough, a lot of school teachers of the non-boarding variety fell into this category.

I can quite understand that you might hate boarding schools if you went to one and disliked it, but there is a huge band of people who hate them for no reason. This might be based on their feelings as parents, but their hate is not usually based on facts or evidence. Some think it demonstrates their superior parenting skills by contrast - look at me, I'm a good parent as I don't pack my children off to school.

I find it strange that people base so much on feelings with nothing to back it up. I also found it very irritating having to constantly defend my love for my boarding school. I found this very early exposure to prejudice served me well for adult life

My parents did not let personal experience dictate their life. They were not like that. My Mum was really terrified of water after her cousin was drowned, and she would not go near the water's edge on a beach, but she encouraged me to go swimming. Both my parents always asked me what I wanted and never told me or decided for me. If I decided that I wasn't going to eat tapioca, that was fine, as long as I had tried it and decided that I didn't like it, despite anyone else thinking it was good for me. There was an awful lot of discussion in our family. In fact we did more discussing than anything else! I cannot remember my parents telling me off much either, they were more likely to offer advice, as that was just how it worked in our family.

I have read a lot about boarding schools. Some people suggest that a boarding school environment produces a hothouse society which can institutionalize children, and that as a consequence they later find it difficult to develop emotional intimacy in adult relationships based on the premise that pupils are organized 24/7 and don't have the distraction of home life. How do people come to this conclusion. You would have to do a very detailed study of a person's life to be able to dismiss so many other factors and put the emphasis and conclusion on just attending a boarding school.

Someone recently said to me that parents who send their children to boarding school are just cruel, and when I asked her to explain her feelings she said 'I don't have any, that is just what I believe and it's true'. That sums it up for a lot of people – they believe what they read or accept things without common sense and question and develop a somewhat irrational opinion. Religion, history and the media have a lot to answer for.

Now, being older, I realise that we do all have our prejudices, some a lot more than others, but it made me wonder how many researchers tend to decide the outcome they want and then try to make the evidence fit, knowing the impact in our media-driven world. Not everything has to be rationalized and one size certainly doesn't fit all. Different children have different needs, so I don't think that we should over analyse and label boarding school as being bad.

Recently a chap from my old school wrote to the 'Brentwood Gazette' in response to the clock tower restoration and the paper's headline was, 'Pupils affectionately remember their time at a state boarding school in Essex'. One of the alumni said, 'It was fun, it was outdoors and I can't remember a bad day'.

I felt I had a duty to tell it as it was, for me. I am in contact with a lot of people I went to school with, and always have been since the day I left Fyfield. We refer to ourselves as 'the Fyfield Family'. This includes teaching and ancillary staff as well as the pupils. Like all families it includes a mix of people; some of them enjoyed their experience and some not. It wasn't a good experience for everyone, but that is true of all schools, whether they are boarding schools or not, and much probably depends on the personality of the person.

One thing I have learnt is that sometimes people who feel they have been bullied at school seem to go through life using it as a reason for other things going wrong with their life, or dwell on it too much to the detriment of moving forward. There was the odd occasion when I felt a bit down about things and I was subjected to the odd bit of bullying, but there were options in dealing with it - ignoring it, getting your own back, just making the bully feel bad it or reporting it, depending on the nature of the crime.

I remember once standing up before the class started and having a real good go at the bully, and I was very surprised at how many people were behind me and told her that her behaviour was disgraceful. Some even said she had tried it with them too, so I had their sympathy. Ignoring it and reporting it were not such good options. We had a school code that said reporting things was not the right thing to do and taking personal responsibility to resolve issues yourself was. One of my friends sent a boy that bullied her parcels of tuck that had been 'altered'.

Nowadays bullying is very different in schools from the way it was in the 1960s. Bullying is not just restricted to school either; it happens in all walks of life, so learning to deal with it yourself is a good skill. But I have known people to say that they are bullied to seek attention or divert attention from something they are doing, especially in working life, and it can be used as an excuse for one's own failings. So I am glad the topic of bullying is now being examined and discussed in schools.

I once looked up the definition of 'boarding school', and to my surprise it did not mention education. The definition was: *a place or environment in which people, especially children, are taught to develop skills and knowledge more quickly than usual.* I like this definition very much. It suits.

Boarding school is not for everybody, but if people opened their minds to finding out more about it they might be pleasantly surprised at what they learn.

State boarding schools have always rated better against state secondary schools when measured by Ofsted. So to mind they cannot be that bad.

A state boarding school differs from other types of boarding school in that the cost of education is met by the state while, for all but the most needy, the boarding costs are paid by parents. My parents paid on a sliding scale. When I first started at school they paid about fifty percent of the fee, but by the time I left they were paying one hundred percent because by this time my father was earning more money. My parents were still in their early 30s when I had finished school.

At Fyfield in the 1960s there were around 240 pupils. It was co-educational, so there were 120 of each sex spread across five years, with two forms per year for the first three years. So there were approximately 24 pupils per class. It was a very small school on a very large site, by today's standards.

My very first impression, on the day I was shown around by two girls who were in the second year of the school, was that this school was a lot nicer than most of the other state schools I'd had the misfortune of either attending or looking at. Perhaps this was because I lived in the East End of London. I went to a day school for almost two terms before joining Fyfield. I had also been to the open days of another three schools in London. There were quite a lot of differences, one being that Fyfield had very small pupil numbers and another was the size of the site and location and the most amazing facilities it had.

Quite a lot of the Fyfield buildings had recently been completed in a modern 1960s style, and it had a swimming pool and a very large playing field too. It seemed a very big site with a lot of buildings to a ten-year-old. It also had a library, and libraries had already played a big part in my life, so my eyes lit up when I saw this. The buildings seemed to be light and airy and had magnificent views from the windows across open countryside wherever you went. Unlike some of the other schools I had seen and the secondary school I had previously attended, it had dedicated rooms for some subjects, like music and art.

My very first memory of the secondary school I went to for just two terms prior to going to Fyfield was that there were hundreds more pupils and as I was small, when the bell went for a change of lessons, bigger, quicker children pushed past me and I was often just crushed in the mêlée of activity. Then, arriving at the next classroom late, I was punished. I didn't remember the teacher's name, only that he had a cane and would use it at every opportunity. Nobody had heard of equality of opportunity or respect - it was survival of the fittest, loudest and brashest. You had art and music in your form room, which also doubled as a changing room for Physical Training (PT or PE as it is now known). It was a very old Victorian building with thick pebble windows that were so high you couldn't see out of them. It was like being imprisoned, and my only relief was going home for lunch. (This was after the first week I started there and had all my dinner money stolen.)

It was very different during my first week at Fyfield. In the beginning sometimes children were homesick, but I wasn't. I made friends straight away and teachers were helping with everything; every little problem you had, a teacher would help you get it resolved. The Headmaster was smiling and walking around telling us there were no rules - that was until the following morning at assembly, when you were given a long list of 'guidelines', which you were expected to follow, as those who were funding your education would be bitterly disappointed if you were found not adhering to his guidelines. He was always around to provide clarification on his guidelines too. During that very first week I knew that the apron (a curved tarmac area) and garden were out of bounds, but he hadn't mentioned the little wall that divided the apron and garden, so I was tiptoeing around this little wall when he came out to ask what I was doing and I just said I was walking on the wall. He said 'But it is out of bounds' and I said, 'Well yes the apron is and the garden is, but you never said about the wall'. He said 'Come here', and I said 'I can't it is out of bounds and now I can't turn around'. So he came and lifted me off the wall and put me down in a place that wasn't out of bounds and said, 'Diane you will have to learn a bit about common sense, but that comes when you get a bit older'. I asked him if I was going to get told off and he just laughed and said 'No, you will learn'. From that moment I trusted him.

I also remember him telling me that there was no such thing as boredom, one just had to try things to find out what it was that would stop me being bored as there was plenty to try, and when I told him I wasn't good at anything he just said 'Well obviously you haven't tried enough to find something you like'. Then he asked his wife to help me find that something, which she did. I had this feeling that he must often have delegated things to his wife. They were a very good team. He had a will to get things done and she had compassion and a motherly understanding. I told her my interest was chatting, so she sat me at her kitchen table and chatted away, mostly about baking. From that moment on I knew I belonged.

Looking back, it seems that the one thing most Fyfield pupils agree on is that it made us independent in many ways. It also gave some of us a sense of adventure, as we were encouraged to give anything a go, no matter how bad we were at the beginning. You didn't have to be good at things - you had to enjoy them.

There was no emphasis on academia, and I wonder whether it is better to develop a range of life skills because enjoyment in what you do is important, not necessarily what you later earn or your job title. I found having qualifications was only useful to open doors to what I wanted and not an end in itself.

Perhaps I just liked Fyfield in contrast to my previous school, or perhaps I decided that I'd give it a go. I'm glad I did.

Developing confidence and independence

Always the argument is about whether boarding is good for children or not. In my opinion, like just about everything else in life, it depends on the people involved. You cannot say categorically something is good or bad, as there is a huge area of grey in this topic.

Many of the people I was at school with and others that went to the same school say it gave us all independence. It made us think for ourselves. It made us explorers. It made us players too. Some people would disagree that this is a good thing. Personally I like independence and like to have my own strong opinions. I think it makes you more interesting than what I refer to as the 'yes' people. These are generally the people who are frightened to be absent in case things change and they become unsettled. You get them at work, in small villages, in sporting organisations. They are made up of people who have to be accepted and fit in and worry if they don't. They suffer a lot of inner turmoil. They even make friends with people they don't really like, just in case. I've never really been keen on fence sitters, preferring people who are tenacious and similar to myself. I think there are far more important things in life than acceptance and being liked.

I did feel a little lost when I left school and started work, but everything was different, the environment, the people, the routine and not having anyone around or near that I knew. I was very young at fifteen to fit into an adult world. I had three jobs before I chose a job and made it a career. Fyfield enabled me to start an interesting career and build on what I had already learnt. Very early on in my occupation I was credited with being able to 'think outside the box', analyse things very methodically, carefully and rationally, have very good personal organisational skills and be able to appreciate other people's opinions, even those completely opposite to my own.

I also developed a lot of confidence, which allowed me not to be browbeaten by authority, control freaks or those who think they can speak for others, rather than just themselves. I built enormous resilience and learnt to argue in a reasonable manner. I developed a very good sense of humour and wit - which not everybody understands, apparently.

When I was young in the 1970s, I learnt that good behaviour, a tidy appearance and an engaging personality can help you to achieve. Fyfield taught me to try hard, to do my best and accept responsibility. I wasn't exceptional at anything, but I was good enough to be able to diversify and try many roles.

Looking back, as far as an academic education was concerned I was young for my age. I sat my GCEs and CSEs, left school and started work when I was 15. I obtained a very average range of results. It wasn't until some years later that I took more GCEs, then studied for a City and Guilds, followed by a whole range of further qualifications. I am sure we all learn at our own pace and in our own time and mine just wasn't at Fyfield as far as qualifications were concerned, but it did teach me a whole range of very good life skills.

I know that like me, a lot of the students who left Fyfield went on to develop careers, as some of them are now psychologists, nurses, teachers, policemen or lawyers, or have their own companies.

It wasn't that Fyfield was at fault in any way - it was a mix of things. Firstly, in the early 1970s having a job was expected until you were married, but building a career was not yet widely accepted for a girl. In any case if children came along it was not considered appropriate to have a career as well, except for a few professions. At Fyfield, like many other secondary schools, suggested careers for girls were often not that inspiring. After all you were not going to be doing it for that long! I remember until then that arguments about career versus motherhood were prominent in the media. It was generally considered that you might do one or the other, but not both and definitely not at the same time. The 1970s saw the start of society's acceptance of working mothers.

Boys had far more attention paid to their careers, and it was considered more important for them. Most of the careers talks at Fyfield in 1969 were for the boys. I remember that one girl wanted to join the police force, and what a discussion there was when she asked to join the careers talk. However, she did.

There wasn't equality of opportunity or equal pay when I left school; these came much later. There was a lot of discrimination, and often girls were asked at interview whether or not they intended to get married and have a child, which was not something I had considered at fifteen. I was always partly embarrassed and partly surprised by this question. It was one of the things that attracted me to the Civil Service, which had a pay scale that did not discriminate too much. The only categories were a junior scale for those under 21 and then a National Scale for those over 21, but men and women earned the same.

An education is so much more than passing exams; it is more about preparing you for life by giving you skills and knowledge that you need. I think Fyfield did that. Exams open doors to enable you to progress, but nowadays you are expected to learn throughout your career, whereas when I left school it was considered almost the end of studying.

Further useful skills and knowledge I needed after leaving Fyfield included shorthand and typing. Shorthand because it is a skill that enables you to write a lot more quickly, and this was handy for my own personal use. Typing because it was rumoured that someone was developing a 'computer', so anyone who knew their way around a keyboard would be sought after. I also learnt to drive a car at seventeen.

After this I wanted a promotion, but I needed one more O level, so I went to night school to get it. The rule was you had to sit them in blocks of four and not one, so I put my name down for three other subjects, none of which I had studied, but to my amazement I managed to get four O levels at the first attempt. This happened another three times, until I had all I needed and moved on to more specialized qualifications because, by this time I had settled into my career.

The hardest exam I sat was when working for HM Customs and Excise. It was hard because I had to remember a lot of information and there was no waffling or getting it nearly right, it had to be precise, verbatim. In my class there were nine men and me. I passed, along with four of the men. The uniform we were given was lovely! It was that which partly enticed me to study hard, but more than that, it was returning to my station to say I had passed, something not expected. I returned with no expression and everybody said 'never mind, you will get another go, no girls have passed it yet from here, so don't worry'. I waited until break time and then Sellotaped my pass note to the door. We celebrated for a week. I have never since drunk that much alcohol. It taught me a real life lesson - never to go drinking with colleagues (the old water guard), the medical profession (the visiting GPs) and pilots.

I continued to build my very enjoyable career. I worked in the Cabinet Office until 2008 and on leaving moved to the North of Scotland.

Even now I still study for enjoyment. It becomes a habit.

Chapter Nine

FYFIELD REMEMBERED

Friends

In all my years at Fyfield there wasn't really anyone I hated. I liked most of the girls in the same year. I don't know why, but it really had never occurred to me to divide anyone into categories of like and dislike, and nobody ever did anything to make me feel I ought to, except one who constantly hid my soap, threw away my toiletries and generally made a nuisance of herself. She was always insulting towards me too, and I avoided her as much as I possibly could. Keeping out of the way was my tactic, and it worked, as we were not in any of the same study groups and she left just as my final year started. In 1970, my very last year at Fyfield there, were eighteen of us left.

Occasionally I had a bout of envy. One of the younger girls was packing her case, as she was going abroad on holiday to a hotel in Majorca and I remember thinking 'oh lucky you'. I asked her lots of questions about it and she didn't know anything about it other than it was hot, it had a swimming pool and she had to fly there. She didn't really want to go, and I thought I'd have given anything to swap places. I'd only been to Clacton and the Isle of Sheppey, although my mind had wandered all over the world, courtesy of the National Geographic magazine.

Another girl had lots of perfumes and potions in jars that covered a whole bookcase, and I was a little envious of her range of cosmetics, so one day I decided to try them for myself without asking. I got caught and told off in no uncertain terms. I had to apologise, but I really liked her, so I really was very sorry. She said she would have let me anyway had I asked her, so this made me feel very bad.

One girl went riding when she went home and that was something I had always wanted to do, not because I specifically wanted to ride, but because I loved animals.

One of my friends, when she left, gave me her Mary-Jane shoes which I had 'borrowed' the whole term, and I was over the moon with that act of kindness. I never knew why she left early, but I am still in contact with her.

I remember some of the girls had musical talent, others had needlework skills and some were very good at sport. I was still good at reading and pretty mediocre at practically everything else, although I did get into the school hockey team as a reserve and played a few matches. Considering there were only eighteen of us left and a few were injured and there had to be eleven in the team, plus a goalie, you might guess that I was pretty lucky to get to play, as I was not a gifted player!

A lot of us were concerned about how tall we were, what we were wearing and who liked who, especially with regard to boys. Fashion and hairstyle was more important to us than how much we weighed. Perhaps that was because we were all mostly the same weight - eight stone something or other.

My best asset was being a good reliable helper, which really didn't stand out as anything special, although I learnt much later on that one of the boys said that I had helped him with a maths problem and he had a crush on me. He even came to visit me once after leaving school, on a Saturday, and still I had no idea of his crush. He was too shy to say and I was too shy to ask! I never saw him again, but in 2012 we re-established contact by email and I laugh about it now, because I really hadn't any clue. I've never much picked up on signals and it would account for why people rightly assume I would be the last to know anything.

Over the years I have been in contact with a few members from my class at school. In 2010 I met up with Angela, who came on a visit to the UK. We spent a few days together in London and I met some of her family, including her two grandchildren. We thought neither of us had changed that much and still got on really well. We had a day out, walking around St James Park, shopping, going to the theatre, eating out and having another meal in. We had a very pleasant time and we now often correspond.

I saw Carole when she came on holiday near to where I

live and we met up and had some lunch together. We have both had very different lives, but I really enjoyed listening to everything she had done, especially in her wilder days when she had just left school. She had some very interesting accounts of what she has done and where she has been. We met for a second time in 2013 and had another lovely lunch. We are going to meet up again in 2015. She is far more outgoing than I am and has a bubbly personality, which is how I remember her from school. She said the first thing she remembered about me was that I was good and not often in trouble at school. More likely I never got caught doing much wrong, but mostly Matron kept me so busy there wasn't time to get into trouble!

I also had Steve, who was in my brother's year, and his partner to lunch not so long ago. We got on very well and he made me laugh a lot. I asked him why my brother took the cat's eye and whether or not he remembered. He said cat's eyes were just lying around at the side of the road, so picking one up was normal, but there was some kudos in who got the biggest and best items when out on a school trip. I said I didn't think the girls did that. It also accounted for why my brother returned to school with an anchor! Later that month I also saw my brother, who I hadn't seen for the past twelve years, and he said 'Oh yes, I do remember that'. I got into big trouble.

For a fairly long period of time during the 80s I was a VAT Senior Officer and went to Ongar and Fyfield on many an occasion to check the records of traders in the area. Traders were often surprised when I told them that I had been to Fyfield Boarding School. I did go into the church and also the village shop, neither of which had changed that much. I also sat, one lunchtime, down by the river in Ongar, but it is a lot busier now. It was quite nice to finally know what was behind some of those walls in Fyfield village. The Gypsy Mead was still up and running, but looking very dated. I think it had become an Indian restaurant. I also had occasion to visit what was referred to locally as the 'posh house', by the river. It was splendid.

I have always been in contact by email with one guy from my year who shares my passion for photography, and we have the same sense of humour. We ask about each other's families, talk about the weather, look at each other's photographs and send each other silly amusing snippets of topical information, mostly political or a daft take on a serious subject. I've chatted to a few others and swapped stories and learnt about their families. It has been great to catch up with some people via social media too.

I returned to school for the second time since leaving some time after it was a housing estate which must have been in the early 2000s. It still had the same feel to it, despite most of the buildings being demolished. The entrance and field seemed to be much the same. The old oak tree that I remember sitting under on hot sunny days was still there and more magnificent. The Art room looked the same despite being made into accommodation. I was quite pleased about that, being one of my favourite places.

In 1985 by chance I met one of the teachers who had been at Fyfield. I was at a natural childbirth talk and I didn't know anyone locally as I worked. It was being held in a village close to where I was living. I went in and took a seat and there right next to me was a face I recognised. We were both expecting our babies around the same time. We politely swapped information about each other, listened to the talk and went our separate ways. Some years later I met her again and I realised that her son and mine were in the same class at grammar school. From then on we saw one another at every parents' evenings and exchanged pleasantries.

So from the original class, I'm still in touch with Christine Ward, Angela, Christine Sturrock, Derek, Mark and Carole, Sylvia, Richenda, Jane, Penny, another Jane (who says she can't remember me at all at school), Janice and Jean. I did have a catch-up with Janice on the phone one day too. Every day social media allow us to communicate with one another in our family group.

Unfortunately I learnt via a friend of the death of Christine Pursley. I was saddened by that because she and I were in one little corner of the dormitory Queens 1 during the last term at school. She was really a lovely person and we got on with one another very well. I will remember her as being very thoughtful and kind.

I reproduce here part of a tribute to Christine published in the Houston Chronicle:

CHRISTINE DIANE WINSLET (PURSLEY), beloved wife of Mark, passed away peacefully on Monday January 30 2006 at the Memorial Hermann Southwest Hospital in

Houston, Texas, following a very brave battle with cancer. Christine was born in a British Army Hospital in Benghazi, North Africa. As the daughter of a colonel in the British Army, her childhood years were spent moving between England, Germany and Singapore. She attended Fyfield Boarding School in England then continued her education at Kingston Management School. Following this, she made her home in London. In 1990 she married Mark and moved to Canada. For the next 16 years, they lived in Calgary, Austin, Jakarta, and finally Sugar Land. Christine will be sorely missed by everyone she touched with her kindness, fun and generosity. A celebration of Christine's life will be held on Saturday, at 11am , February 2nd 2006 at 3:00pm in the chapel of the Settegast-Kopf Co. in Sugar Land.

It would be fair to say though that there is a whole community of Fyfieldians that includes people and teachers, through a couple of social media sites. Some of them also meet up at old school reunions and some, like me, still have their own little network of old schoolfriends. A couple of my friends have tried to encourage me to go to the reunions and I know they really enjoy them, but I think I'd like to just remember the days at school, the way it was. Summed up, that would be sitting on the field in sunshine with the smell of newly-mown grass, eggy bread for breakfast, the noise from the swimming pool, walking around the perimeter of the field after midnight, crisp crunchy frost underfoot after winter prep and school council banter.

Chapter Ten

OLD FYFIELDIANS LOOK BACK

Underwear and wood polish

I remember waiting outside Ilford Town Hall for the double decker bus. It arrived, looming over us; children said their goodbyes to various people. I boarded the bus after saying a fond goodbye to my aunt. I had my sister with me; she was in the fifth year and was an old hand at this.

We went upstairs, staring down at the people below and frantically waving at my aunt. I clutched on to the panda she had just given me; I wasn't going to let that go! The journey to school was a long one, but it was taken up by singing various songs about school and the headmaster. I expect I had fallen asleep by the time we arrived; my sister took me through to Sommerville dorm. This was a huge long room with beds, chest of drawers, wardrobes and bedside cabinets.

A lot of information was bombarded into our heads! We were taught how to strip the bed every morning and fold the bedding, remaking the bed with hospital corners. Then the period talk came, and people started put up their hands. Oh goodness, then out came the Dr Whites - we could get them from Sick Bay; Matron would wrap them in newspaper so no one knew what they were! Of course, as my family were all keen swimmers, I was already using tampons - shock horror! So began my not so great relationship with Matron.

One of my memories was the bizarre ritual of hanging our underwear at the end of the bed. It had to be one pair of knickers, one pair of socks (long and grey) and your vest. Regardless of whether you wore a bra or not, that vest was to be hanging on the end of the bed. I didn't wear vests, so I had one that was hung up every night for a year or two!

I have many happy memories of my time at Fyfield, friends, teachers, lessons and sport. I hope my first true love still remembers me! I loved all sport, playing for my house and competing against other schools. There was early morning swimming, tumble turns, continuous relays and also the sponsored swim.

Returning back to Fyfield for the next new term, I loved the smell of wood polish on the dorm's floors, a smell that said 'welcome back'. Often on visiting weekends when we went home I would stay, as there were a number of children who could not go home. We played volleyball and ate in the same part of the dining room, usually in our house section.

During the autumn and winter terms the school day was broken up. We had lessons in the morning, then dinner, after-school clubs, tea time, then back to lessons in the early evening, then on to supper, then into prep, a bit of free time then back to the dorm. During the lighter months lessons returned to normal times.

We had lessons Monday to Friday just like any school, but then we would have prep every night. On Saturday mornings we had prep too, then the rest of the day was free, with maybe a film in the evening or a dance. Sunday morning you either went to church or had prep. After dinner it was inter-house games, and if you were not playing then you were on the sidelines cheering.

After tea came the letter writing, just to make sure everyone wrote to their families. Next was the school assembly, when we sat on our school chairs, which we had to carry from our classrooms. I still bear the scars of one those times - the chairs had metal legs and the rubber bung in the bottom sometimes came out!

There was an assembly every day, but we just stood for that. This was mainly for daily notices to be read out. In the evenings you could gather in your common room and play games, or just hug a radiator and chat.

As the school had about 240 children, we all knew each other, and the teachers also took on the roles of Dorm Masters or Mistresses. I loved this as I had come from a primary school with just under 125 pupils. In this day and age these numbers could just represent one school year!

Routine was high on the school's list, and punishment

was also handed out from black marks to the slipper or worse, the cane. Now as I am older I wonder what the staff actually thought of the more excessive punishments. For talking after lights out there were different punishments which were usually done by the prefect of your dorm - holding pillows out on your arms, running round the quad or even the school field.

As I progressed through the school, I came to think of Fyfield with great fondness, as I still do today. If I had my time there again I wouldn't change anything I did - maybe a few things, but for the most part no. I ended up as Head of House for Berners; I got a swimming record in my first year that still stood when I left. In my last year we won the Swimming Gala and also broke the relay record. I received school colours for hockey and won many sports and swimming races.

The same could not be said for my education, but this has not stopped me achieving other educational things since. Many of my teachers would now say about me 'Yes, always in a daydream'. There are so many things I could write about Fyfield, but I have been given just a little precious space for my thoughts.

- Christine Sturrock.

Spots and Freckles

Why is it that when you get to a certain age you become aware of particular physical things about your body which others find amusing? The staff nickname for me was 'Spotty

Dog'. I assume this was from the Woodentops on Watch with Mother. When I was admitted to Sick Bay with German measles my face was covered with both freckles and red spots. At this point l thought l had killed a robin, as two days further on l started to itch with chicken pox. Matron, as expected, could not believe my bad luck. So the face really was not a pretty sight.

Old Fyfield pupils who spent any time in Sick Bay may remember that Matron did have an evening off. Staff took it in turns to sit in with the pupils. I remember hearing Matron say that they must not speak about the state of my face, due to the high spot count. When the staff members came into the room they looked at me and really struggled to speak. They had to ask Matron what my name was. As my name had completely vanished from their memory l was 'Spotty Dog' in more ways than one!

- Christine Ward (Christine Bridge, 1965-1970)

Beating at a Shoot

During the winter terms some boys were either chosen or asked to be included in a list for beating at a shoot - this happened quite regularly and was regarded as an honour.

Early on the day a vehicle would arrive at school, and the lucky ones would be carted off to some set of woods out in the sticks. The morning would be spent walking in rows and with sticks, through fields, copses and woods, beating bushes and yelling to get the birds in the air – though we were cold and often wet and weary, it actually was great fun with the shooters enjoying the out-and-about bit as much as the pupils.

I vaguely remember lunches, often in a barn, with sandwiches and sausage rolls and soup - and if the shooters were generous, a nip from a flask.

The afternoon section was similar, but the real thrill was being transported back to one of the shoot members' houses and being fed huge meals before being transported back to school.

Land Rovers full of feathered carcasses would be divided up after the final beat, often quite a few dozen of them. I don't recall every being given any to take back to school though.

It was an excellent way to spend a Sunday.

- Simon Humphries

Football

While we were watching a televised football match in one of the rooms around the quadrangle - I think it was the music room for some reason and could have been part of the '66 world cup matches - England scored - and all the boys in the room erupted, until one unfortunate boy seized a chair to wave above his head and promptly put the chair leg through one of the bulbs up above, resulting in broken glass showering down across the room. The whole atmosphere became a lot more subdued very rapidly.

Cricket

Often some of the senior pupils were asked to join the village cricket team at weekends. As the School Caretaker was part of the team, this resulted in more 'awaydays' and was appreciated. One fateful game, a win for the village team, resulted in a celebration at a public house where the pupils were sometimes allowed a 'proper' drink. After one of these matches I recall being woken in the dormitory late at night to see a fellow player/pupil being carried out by an ambulance crew to have his stomach pumped. Restrictions came in very quickly after this incident!

The Easter tour of Austria

I never went on this trip but I will tell you about it anyway, as one contributor to my book has written about the start of the trip. I did visit Austria in the early 70s and I have been to the places that the people on this trip visited.

The group left on a Thursday morning, 27th March 1970, and arrived at their destination some time on Friday afternoon, having travelled by train, boat and finally an overnight coach to reach their final destination of the Gasthof Kendl in Salzburg. The Saturday was spent in Salzburg, where the group were taken all around the conventional sites such as the Cathedral and the location where the Sound of Music was filmed.

They visited Hellbrunn, is a large baroque villa built by Markus Stittikus von Hohnems, Prince-Archbishop of Salzburg 1613-19. It was built as a summer residence, but it was not used during the night, so it has no bedrooms. It is quite famous for the water games which are built secretly into the gardens, apart from one small place where the Archbishop used to sit. It attracts many visitors, and I was one in the early 1970s. It was reported that the cleverly-concealed water jets were pointing at those on the trip and without warning, out shot the water and many of them got wet.

The pupils then went in a cable car to a mountain top, where they threw snowballs, and then to a little village outside Salzburg to see a folklore festival. Then they moved to Vienna, where some of the group visited the Spanish Riding School, whilst others visited a fine arts gallery or went swimming. Later, the whole group visited the Schönbrunn Palace, where apparently their over-enthusiastic guide indicated that everything was beautiful or most beautiful. I understand the whole of the group got a tad fed up with this, despite her knowledge of the subject, which they found very interesting.

Later they visited the Prater, the funfair in Vienna. They rode on the big wheel, go carts and dodgems. They also drove through the Vienna Woods, where they visited an underground lake and viewed the castle where the film Frankenstein was made. They also viewed the imperial hunting lodge at Mayerling and learnt of the Mayerling incident, a series of events which led to the apparent murder or suicide of Crown Prince Rudolf of Austria, which had momentous consequences for the course of history.

The final event in their trip was a visit to Grinzing, where they took part in some wine tasting, but it was reported that despite the cellar being renowned for its wine, it tasted to them more like vinegar.

They returned the following Friday, having spent a most enjoyable week there. This is a further account of the trip by one of my classmates, Christine, who did go on the trip.

"If l remember correctly, travelling to Austria via a bus in the late 60s was not the most comfortable way, but when a friend gets toothache just outside Paris you really need help. I'm sure even in those days it was illegal to give minors strong painkillers. I remember a female staff member putting cotton wool in my friend's mouth and telling her to leave it against her tooth. This process was repeated numerous times. I remember how she began to hum songs, then became quite loud. And the cotton wool kept coming down the bus. On arrival she struggled to get off the bus and fell down in the snow. It was Easter in Salzburg.

She was still laughing as she was taken off to a local dentist without a care in the world. So what was going on? Cotton wool would not have removed toothache, would it? But cotton wool soaked in whiskey would! The sound of clinking duty-free bottles from the back of the bus was really a dead giveaway. If only l had toothache too! So thank you again to the staff of Fyfield for your knowledge and skill in turning pain into pleasure, and possibly the experience of alcohol-induced pain relief which l used later on in life!

Definitely not politically correct! But at least she did enjoy the trip after a visit to the dentist, and so did l. Salzburg was great fun in the snow. Vienna? Possibly not for a group of our age. But I'm sure some enjoyed it.

- Christine Ward

Sounds of Fyfield

I know it might be unusual to associate noise with boarding school, but there are a few distinct sounds which evoke memories of my time at Fyfield. One was the sound of the grass being cut on the enormous school field and the associated smell of new grass, which created both a soothing sound and a sensuous smell. It was the sound of a summer's day, a long hot summer's day when time seemed to expand to keep the day alive. The sound of a summer's evening when you heard the cricket ball hitting the bat. When the sun was setting and the dew was forming, a lovely warm damp smell of newly-cut grass escaped into the night air from that playing field.

The school bell was situated between the dining room and quadrangle. It was a large bell and people were dispatched to ring it to signal events during the day. I remember this so well because the bell had a different sound according to who was ringing it. When teachers or the Headmaster rang it, it took on an authoritative tone. When a male prefect rang it, it sounded loud and impatient, and when it was a female prefect, it was sweet and soft. You could almost tell the time by the ringing of the bell, as it was hardly ever late, though occasionally it was early.

The dining room noise of the cutlery and crockery being cleared from the tables and the sound of the industrial dishwasher produced an ongoing cacophony, and when it had died down you knew that next there would be messages to pupils. It started with a light sound and rose to a crescendo before tailing off again. Who would have thought that 234 children all talking could create such a noise? The very last sound was chairs being scraped across the dining room floor.

Early morning music. The first out of bed put on the very small transistor radio. If it was your favourite song, you wanted to stay and listen to it, which resulted in a dash to the washroom as soon as it finished. If you really liked the second record, it signalled being late for breakfast, unless you were really disciplined. Music too came from the music room when a group of would-be musicians decided that practising all at the same time would be good a good idea. The different tunes and different key formed a very odd, unsettling sound.

The never-ending sound of the extractor fans in the drying room. Even from other rooms around the quadrangle, the extractor fan noise rang out to fill the space. It was a constant regular hum. This went quite well with the noise of the chatter from the payphone in the little cold cubbyhole between Somerville and the washroom.

There was the noise that emanated from the swimming pool. All the time it was in use, it sounded like a noise cocooned in a plastic box. I suppose that's what it was, a mixture of splashing, swimming and shouting with the occasional whistle blowing for some misdemeanour.

In the early days I remember the noise on a winter's morning of the carrion crows, a very distinctive loud noise that carried on the quiet early morning air. Very early, if my memory serves me well. I say it was the early days, as I seem to remember that the noise stopped at one point. The crows were in a row of trees towards the village a few hundred yards from the school.

Chapter Eleven

AFTER FYFIELD

I left Fyfield in the June of 1970 and spent a couple of weeks with my friend Jean, first staying with her and then she stayed with me. This greatly helped me to get used to Southend. It was not a place I really liked, but Jean and I explored the town and found all the positive elements - the pier, the seafront and the library. It also had a couple of department stores, a bus station and two train stations. It wasn't dull, but it wasn't familiar.

I tried one or two jobs, but I never really settled into them. My parents encouraged me to do my first job at fifteen years old, as it would be good for me. It was at Post Office Telephones. I was there for about a year. I loved it, but I grew out of it because it was repetitive and I wanted something better paid and more exciting.

I worked in an office and then at the Southend Telephone Exchange. I liked the telephone exchange, despite working mainly on my own. The best part of this job was that I spoke to other telephone operators and asked them all about where they were located. This made me actually both interested and fairly good at identifying the geographical locations of cities and towns throughout Europe and the UK. Frankly I was in my element with all those connections and cords at the main exchange. It lasted until the exchange went automatic with standard telephone dialling, when they decided I should return to work in the office calculating timesheets for engineers' pay. It was so repetitive that I only stayed another two weeks. If the switchboard work had continued, I would have stayed, but it was not to be.

The second job a teacher at school told me about; it was in a drawing office at Basildon Development Corporation. I wasn't really old enough to settle in and working with an all-male staff was really not good for a girl of 16. I took the job because the pay was double what I had previously earned, but I was lonely, disruptive, and unhappy. Eventually I left because I was demotivated, as there just wasn't enough work for me to do and people shouted a lot. I think it was the only job I really hated, and I couldn't find anything positive at all about it. I vowed never to take a job as a general factotum again.

The men shared a camaraderie, and I felt excluded. They were very pleasant to me, but the environment was alien. To make matters worse they went out and left me to sit in an empty office to take messages, should there be any. It was in the middle of nowhere at a place called Bowers

Gifford. I stuck it for nine months or so, but I just felt as if I was treading water, time was passing and it held little interest for me. I became very stressed with the job, so decided to call it a day after I found that the girl who was photocopying was getting double my wage. It was really good, because it made me really focus on what I should do next. I was coming up seventeen.

The following week I took a temporary job at a local mail order factory. I thought I would earn some money before trying to get into what I really wanted to do, but at that time I didn't know what that was. Funnily enough, the job was exceptionally well paid and I had plenty of overtime too, so I managed to build up considerable savings during this short window of six months. It paid for my driving lessons. Not only that but I met a great crowd of people working in the warehouse, which included lots of trainee teachers and students.

The best part of the job was working in a good team with fair division of duties and everyone helping each other out. The oddest part was answering the telephone from members of the public on the enquiries desk, where I managed to speak to some pretty weird people asking totally irrelevant questions about the underwear catalogue. This was an education in itself. However, the skill I took from this was that no matter how amused you might be, you have to try and stay professional at all times. I also managed to develop a plethora of regional accents and many animal noises when answering the phone, which alleviated tedium for a short while and amused those I worked with. I can identify with a current TV programme called 'The Call Centre', because people on the phone can well and truly test your patience. This job was good in so much as it opened my eyes to all sorts of opportunities and the trainee teachers who manned the warehouse, waiting for their first teaching posts, were a very good group of people to work with. There was nothing nicer than teachers who hadn't yet taught children.

The trouble was that I didn't understand what careers were open to me or even how to get an interesting job, so I went along to the Southend Labour Exchange, where they were pushing the Civil Service, as the new Value Added Tax centre was being built in Southend and they needed a lot of staff. I decided I could probably do OK in the Civil Service, as you could move around from department to department, and up to this point monotony and simplicity of work were my main problems. I failed to understand why nobody gave any responsibility or anything that required intelligence to a young person. It was almost like being a servant, but in the office environment.

So I joined the Civil Service on January 1st 1973, appointed to Her Majesty's Customs and Excise. That was before January 1st was declared a public holiday. I had been out the night before, had far too much to drink and spent my first whole day in a new job with a hangover feeling queasy and hoping that the day would end so I could go home. It was my induction day and I learnt nothing. I sat in a room with lots of people of the same age, all of us looking bored. The HR had arranged for various speakers of the different societies and the Union, which meant nothing whatsoever to any of us.

Day two was better. I was allocated to a Department called Credibility, the meaning of which is 'the quality of being trusted and believed in', which after day one, seemed quite amazing really.

I was dealing with Purchase Tax in the beginning and then moved onto developing checks to see whether or not the very first VAT returns seemed credible. Everything was mathematically based, so my interest was awakened. Age did not come into the equation regarding responsibility, it was all down to whether or not when tested you could carry out the required functions. I was considered to be ahead of the game.

Most of the returns that did not appear credible in those days were because traders had difficulty in understanding how to fill the forms in and a lot of my time was spent in explaining that.

One day the Head of Personnel decided that everyone under the age of 21 must go to study at the technical college across the road to better themselves. This was a brilliant opportunity for me as we could take three subjects, which I did, two academic and one non-academic. So straight away I signed up for Modern Mathematics, Accounts and Yoga. Not only that, it meant less time at work, and that meant less time listening to those a bit older than me moaning about their jobs. At this point life could hardly get better.

I then spent 28 years with HM Customs and Excise, doing a variety of diverse jobs, some in VAT and some in uniform at an airport or at the docks boarding ships, some at Headquarters developing policy and strategy on drugs enforcement. I was also given the opportunity to carry out many projects and one-off jobs, some exciting. I worked in many places and had plenty of highlights to my career. Throughout my time there I had many wonderful opportunities and plenty of excitement, and I met some very lovely people too. At Customs they were like a family.

I then took a job as a developmental opportunity at the Cabinet Office in Whitehall, although when the chance and an opening arose, I decided to stay. I worked in the Women's Unit, then the Women and Equality Unit, and lastly the Civil Contingencies Secretariat part of the Intelligence Security and Resilience Division, and I undertook a variety of projects too. Once again I enjoyed my time there and had many opportunities.

In 2004 I had to undergo treatment for cancer, and it sapped all my strength so much that although I carried on working for another four years, everything was becoming far more difficult for me, both at work and with travelling, because the Olympic Village was being built on my commuting route, which meant that trains were getting overcrowded, so consequently the journey became difficult and tiring. I decided to leave and handed in my notice in 2007 and left in 2008. Another incentive was that my husband had already retired early and I wanted to share time with him.

So at the end of 2009, after 38 years in the Civil Service, I moved to Scotland. Everyone asks why. A lot of people come on holiday and then decide to move here, but this was not so for me. It was pure economics and a desire to leave the very crowded south east of the UK. In fact I had only spent a few days in the area, and that had been out of chance. The air was clean, I found a little house with a nice sea view and above all I thought the little rescued cat, Soda, would like it. The first my husband saw of it was the day we moved in.

And that is where my next story begins.

Appendix

EXAM RESULTS

I have arranged my results based on the marking system for GCSE 2014.

A*   English Language
      Additional English Studies
      (now called Media Studies)

A   Modern Mathematics
      Human Biology (resit of the previous one)
      English Literature
      Accounts

B   Medieval History
      Geography
      Mathematics
      English Language

Domestic Science
Domestic Science 2 (included childcare)
Human Biology
Music

C   Biology
Art and Craft

Where you see the same subject, it was different course material and taken in a different year at a different place.

Later on I completed various City and Guilds, then degrees, in HR subjects and Management. I became a Licentiate Member of the Chartered Institute of Personnel and Development in 2007. I never really stopped learning and taking exams, throughout my career.

I got to grips with computers in 1984 and found that this really was an area that I enjoyed. Had they been around earlier I would probably have learnt even more about them and their applications. I have recently been able to set my new machine up successfully and manage to play computer games, and have reasonable skill in many applications.

Printed in Great Britain
by Amazon